THE SMALL BRAVE CITY-STATE

EBIEGBERI JOE ALAGOA

THE
SMALL
BRAVE
CITY-STATE

A HISTORY
OF NEMBE-BRASS
IN THE NIGER DELTA

1964

IBADAN UNIVERSITY PRESS, NIGERIA

THE UNIVERSITY OF WISCONSIN PRESS, MADISON

Published in Africa by
Ibadan University Press
Ibadan, Nigeria

Published in North America by
The University of Wisconsin Press
Mailing address: P.O. Box 1379, Madison, Wisconsin 53701
Editorial offices: 430 Sterling Court, Madison

For GBORIBUSUOTE and AYEBATONYE

ACKNOWLEDGMENTS

I wish to acknowledge the beneficient influence I have received from Dr. K. Onwuka Dike, Principal of the University of Ibadan and Director of the National Archives of Nigeria, under the shadow of whose wings I have worked for many years as student and archivist.

I am greatly indebted, too, to Professors Philip D. Curtin and Jan Vansina of the Program in Comparative Tropical History at the University of Wisconsin, who kindly read the manuscript and made valuable suggestions for its improvement, and to the Carnegie Corporation of New York for financial support that made it possible for me to study in the United States. Neither the Carnegie Corporation nor the Program in Comparative Tropical History, however, is responsible for the fact or opinion in the words that follow.

His Highness Francis Osamade Joseph Allagoa, Mingi X, Amanyanabo of Nembe, encouraged me to embark on the project of writing a history of Nembe.

Many local friends helped in various ways: Rev. Isaac Abraham Ockiya (as Teacher Abraham, the man who taught me traditional Nembe history in the infant school), Messrs. J. A. Ombu, S. F. Iyala, J. S. Berena, T. O. Alagoa, Charlie Abaye, J. Alfred Ockiya, S. G. Kpokiri, C. O. Amiebi, L. B. Iyalla, A. E. Evborokhai, and J. O. Zain.

The following persons have done typing jobs for me at different stages of the preparation of the manuscript without asking for any reward: Messrs. Emmanuel Edgar, I. B. Ahaiwe, J. E. Enebeli, E. Bonnie, and Miss C. A. Olali. The Cartographic Laboratory of the University of Wisconsin prepared the maps for this book. I am deeply grateful to all.

Madison, Wisconsin   E. J. ALAGOA
July 1963

ACKNOWLEDGMENTS

NOTE ON TRANSLITERATION

Two vowels (*e, o*) and two consonants (*b, d*) do not always have the same sound value in Nembe. In normal orthography a diacritic is used to indicate the difference.

e without a diacritic is equivalent to the first part of the English diphthong *ei* as in *day*.

ē with a diacritic equals the English vowel in *get*.

o without a diacritic equals the English *o* in molest.

o with a diacritic equals the English vowel in *saw*.

The two plosives, a bilabial *b* and alveolar *d*, become implosives by the addition of a diacritic. The breath is drawn in at the end of the sound. In the case of the implosive *b* or *d*, an apostrophe, in some few cases in the text, has been added after the consonant, as, *B'assam b'iri*, to indicate the pronunciation.

CONTENTS

MAPS · ILLUSTRATIONS

THE SMALL BRAVE CITY-STATE

". . . the town marked as Brass in the maps is incorrectly so named, it being Tuwon, the true Brass Town of white traders, or Nimbe, being thirty-five miles from the sea."

Dr. William Balfour Baikie • 1854

1

INTRODUCTION

The use of the adjectives "small" and "brave" in the title of this book — *The Small Brave City-State* — is a rendering of the traditional praise name of the Brass or Nembe people. The praise name was normally beaten out on the talking drum as the war canoes of Nembe approached a neighboring town or returned home from an adventure. It ran thus:

> Kala Ekulema Nembe [twice]
> Ama doko doko biokpo,

meaning — "Kala Ekule's town Nembe, a tiny town, but stout-hearted." The name of the first king of the whole people was Kala Ekule, and the implication is that Nembe was a small community, but one able to exert great influence in the Niger Delta.

The use of the word "city-state" also has historic interest for the Brass or Nembe people. In his penetrating study of the Niger Delta, Dr. Dike, finding that these communities were organized on the pattern of the Greek city-state,[1] called them city-states. He rejected the term "tribal-state" as applicable to these Delta communities because "citizenship came increasingly to depend not on descent but on residence." The organization of peoples over a wide area around a single city may properly be described as a city-state, and the term is so applied to Nembe and the towns grouped around it.

I shall attempt to tell the story of Nembe from its beginnings, or from about the middle of the fifteenth century and even earlier.[2] Information down to the present is given at many points, but the

3

formal limit of the study is conceived to be about 1936, that is, to the reign of the Reverend Anthony Ockiya, Mingi IX.

Oral sources have been used extensively. Fortunately, most of these oral sources are now recorded and can be found at the National Archives of Nigeria, Enugu and Ibadan (NA/E and NA/I in the notes). A veritable mine of custom and tradition was located by me in an unpublished manuscript by the late Rev. D. O. Ockiya. It is now preserved at the National Archives, Enugu. Another source used was Adebiyi Tepowa, a Yorubaman who had worked at the consulate at Brass and gathered material from local informers. His "History" was apparently first issued as a pamphlet but was later enlarged and published in the *Journal of the African Society* in 1907.[3] Mr. Ockiya, however, was a Nembeman, thoroughly grounded in the traditions of his people, and he had the advantage of being able to check Tepowa's material and his use of a few missionary sources. Mr. Ockiya's dating is accordingly more reliable.

There are only scattered references to Nembe in the works of Talbot, Leonard, and Dike,[4] but these and the traditional sources have been supplemented with the accounts of nineteenth-century explorers and traders. Other sources have been given in detail in the notes.

The paucity of published material on Nembe history does not mean that the subject is without either interest or importance. This work is conceived as a piece of local history that may also be a contribution to the study of Nigerian history and to African society and institutions. It should certainly add to an understanding of the Niger Delta States and to such matters as the extent to which the influence of Benin ran to the eastward.

BRASS

The early European traders found on the rivers Nun, Brass, and St. Nicholas a people who were hard bargainers. They used repeatedly the word "Barasin," meaning "let go" or "leave off"— which indicated a determination not to accept unfair prices. The white traders came to refer to the people as the Barasin people, and the word was finally contracted to Brass. The name was thus applied originally to the people as a whole but was soon extended to their capital city and to the rivers running through the area. The city of Nembe became Brasstown. The River Nun (*Akassa Toru*) was for a time known as the First Brass River. The river originally known to the Portuguese as St. John, Rio Bento, Malfonso, Oddy, and Fonsoady became the Second Brass River or simply the River Brass (*Twon Toru*).[5] The place-name Brasstown or Brass was, in the late nineteenth century, transferred from the metropolitan city of Nembe to Twon on the mouth of the Brass River. This was the place where the oil palm traders established their "factories" or stores and where the British vice-consuls for Brass settled in the last decade of the nineteenth century.

The people call themselves and their capital city Nembe. (They have been called variations of the same name by their immediate neighbors: the Kalabari on the east called it Nimbi; the Ogbia and Osomari — *Aboh* — to the north and northwest made it Itebu; and the Ijaw clans to the west, Debe.) The name may have been that of one of the early kings. There is also a method of fishing called *nembe*[6] and this name may have been transferred to the people.

The town of Nembe or Brasstown is hidden among a number of creeks somewhat to the east of the rivers Brass and St. Nicholas, some thirty miles from the sea. It is divided into two principle sections, Ogbolomab'iri and B'assamb'iri (see Note on Transliteration for diacritical marks), which are separated by a small creek about fifty yards wide. Around these sections are three small suburban settlements — Oromabiri (Juju town), Okipiri, and Tub'opiri (watering bush or bush of wells). In the surrounding country for about sixty miles around are towns and villages looking to Nembe as their mother city and identifying themselves as Nembe. The most important of these are Okpoma ("Fishtown" in the records), Odioma (on the St. Nicholas), and Twon (the "Brass" of modern maps). Twon is composed of a cluster of settlements — the consulate, Imbikiri, Kemmer's town or Oruwarikiri, Twonbio, and Spiff's town or Gbokokiri. On the periphery are other towns and peoples who have come within the Brass city-state at one time or another, but have distinctive features of culture and traditions. These include Beletiema, Diema, Egwema, Okoroba, Idema, Agrisaba, Liama, Akassa, Akipelai, Amakalakala, and Opomatubu. The smaller villages are grouped around the bigger ones and look to Ogbolomabiri and Bassambiri. Most of them look to Ogbolomabiri for leadership but Odioma, Okoroba, Idema, and Agrisaba are more closely attached to Bassambiri.

In 1895 the count of major Nembe towns was sixteen.[7]

1. Ogbolomabiri ⎫ Nembe	6. Obioku	11. Egwema
2. Bassambiri ⎭	7. Diema	12. Liama
3. Okpoma (Fishtown)	8. Fantuo	13. Egenelogo
4. Twon	9. Ewelesuo	14. Sabatoru
5. Odioma	10. Beletiema	15. Etiema
		16. Kirupogo

Even in 1895 there may have been many more small villages: today there would be over double the number of major towns.

There are no reliable early estimates of the size of Nembe, but a government estimate of 1915 gives for the "Brass Division" an approximate area of 3,056 square miles and a population of 96,000. In 1921 a government census puts the population figure at 55,654. No figures were given for the area in the 1931 census, but the 1953 census gives for the Brass Division a total of 126,954 people.[8] The 1953 census split this figure into clan and native administration areas as follows:

Clan and native administration areas	Number of people
Nembe	24,297
Ogbia	20,720
Epie-Atissa	9,335
Eastern Ijaw	72,002

This division represents the main groups into which the people of the Brass Division may be split. The 1953 census also gave figures which we may use as an indication of the comparative size of the major Nembe towns:

Town	Number of people	Town	Number of people
Ogbolomabiri	2,098	Diema	726
Bassambiri	1,623	Egwema	405
Okpoma	2,383	Okoroba	593
Twon	948	Idema	888
Beletiema	161	Agrisaba	214

IJAW TRIBE,[9] CLANS, STATES

The subdivision of the Brass Division into Nembe, Ogbia, Epie-Atissa, and Eastern Ijaw clans indicates some of the ethnic characteristics of the Niger Delta. The major tribe of the Niger Delta is Ijaw and the Brass-Nembe clan sits at the center of the Delta and the tribe. The celebrated Delta States of Dike and others are merely subgroups or clans of the Ijaw tribe. From west to east Brass was the first of the states, the others being New Calabar or Awome (the Kalabari), Okrika, Bonny (Okoloba or Ibani), and Opobo (founded from Bonny in 1870). To the west of Brass are the groups officially designated Eastern and Western Ijaw,[10] and known to the eastern people as Ijaw. These groups to the west of Brass call themselves Ijonotu — Ijoh or Ijo people. They are subdivided into more than twelve clans: Apoi, Bassa, Bomo, Ekpetiama, Gbaran, Ogboin, Oporoma, Opokuma, Okordia, Zarama, Kolokuma, Trakiri, and others.

Talbot may have been the first to apply the name Ijaw to all the peoples in the Delta from the River Forcados to Opobo in the 1920 census of southern Nigeria. The Portuguese referred to the peoples they saw on the Rivers Forcados and Ramos as "Jos," [11] that is, Ijaw, but referred to all others by their distinctive local names. The early British explorers applied the curious name "Oru" to the Ijaw west of Brass from the Nun entrance to Taylor Creek. Dr. Baikie said of them in 1854:

From the mouth of the river [Nun] up to this point [Taylor Creek], the country on either side is named Oru. The people are of the same tribe as those who inhabit the tract of country up to the Rio Formoso, where however they are called Ejo or Ojo, by which name also they are known at Abo, at Brass, and even at Bonny. By English palm-oil traders they are often termed Jo-men. Throughout this district but one language is spoken, with but very little dialectical difference.[12]

Dr. Baikie does not explain where he got the name Oru as the appropriate term for Ijaw. The word means "a God" in Nembe and it is clear the explorer did not get it from a Nembe source. Records at Enugu show that certain peoples in the Orlu and Okigwi areas are called Oru, a name applied in Ibo to waterside people.[13]

In 1906 Major Arthur Glyn Leonard listed a number of "tribes" of the Delta, distinguishing an Oru as well as an Ijo tribe:

The Oru occupy the tract of country on each side of the Nun Branch of the Niger, and along the coastline between it and the Ramos river.

Then in the triangle formed by the Nun and the Gana-Gana, also outside it, to a small extent, both eastward and westward, dwell the Ijo,

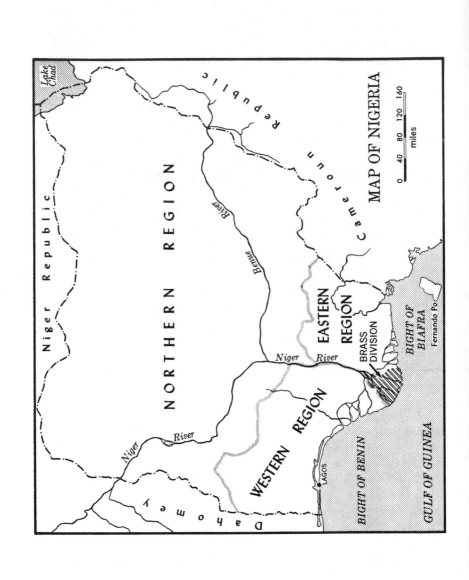

the most important tribe in the lower Delta, and indeed, after the Ibo, in the whole of southern Nigeria.[14]

And while classifying each of the other Delta communities — Ibani (Bonny, Opobo), Okrika, New Calabar (Kalabari), and Brass (Nembe) — as "tribes," Leonard classified their languages as merely "dialects of Ijo."

In classifying the Delta communities together as a single tribe — Ijaw — in 1921, Talbot had also based his conclusion on similarity in language. Talbot observed three main groups of African languages — Bantu, Semi-Bantu, and Sudanic. He classed all the languages of Western Nigeria, the Delta, and the Ibo areas of Eastern Nigeria as Sudanic; the Ibibio and northeastern half of Eastern Nigeria as Semi-Bantu; and the south of the Southern Camerouns as Bantu. According to Talbot

The earliest of all Nigerian languages is Ijaw, which would appear to date back to primeval times — a relic of pure negro speech.[15]

Talbot considered the Ijaw language very isolated, having "not the slightest affinity with any other" in Nigeria, except with Andoni Ibibio and Abuan. The various tongues spoken by the Delta peoples, thus grouped together, Talbot called dialects, and the peoples who spoke them "subtribes and clans." Table 1 is based on the result of Talbot's 1921 census and classification:[16]

TABLE 1

The Ijaw: Their subtribes and clans by sex and as percentage of the tribe

Subtribe	Clan	Male	Female	Total	As percentage of the tribe
Kalabari	Kalabari	37,001	40,468	77,469	45
Lower-Ijaw	Brass-Nembe	6,550	7,066	13,616 ⎱	
	Ogbinya	5,266	5,076	10,342 ⎰ 15	
	Brass-Ijaw	882	886	1,768 ⎰	
Western Ijaw	Warri	26,101	29,902	56,003 ⎱	
	Atissa	1,755	2,041	3,796 ⎰ 36	
	Mini	1,117	1,343	2,460 ⎰	
Unclassified		4,296	4,026	8,322	
Total		82,968	90,808	173,776	

Source: P. A. Talbot, *The Peoples of Southern Nigeria* (London, 1926), IV, 47.

The Ijaw language has not been closely studied by modern African linguists. Westermann and Bryan (1952) based all their comments on Talbot, adding that "no detailed information is available on the dialects and their distribution."[17] Accordingly they were sceptical of all attempts to classify the language and treated it under the head of "isolated language groups and units."

Greenberg[18] classified Ijaw as a subfamily within his Niger-Congo family of African languages. But it is clear that he was equally handicapped by lack of detailed information. No enumeration of the dialects within the subfamily was included, as was done for other subfamilies.

Due to sheer lack of study, Ijaw seems to be moving in the direction of being labeled as inscrutable, isolated — and to being conveniently set aside. Talbot's statement that it did have some affinity with Andoni Ibibio and Abuan is worthy of note. Most of the Ijaw dialects on both sides of Brass are obviously similar, even to the layman, but there are a few that, although situated within the Ijaw geographical area, are strikingly different. These would include Andoni, Abua, Ogbia, Epie-Atissa, Saka, and some very much smaller groups. Andoni and Abua were the groups known to Talbot. Greenberg, probably using Talbot data, put Abua as one of the Cross River languages in the Central Branch subfamily of the Niger-Congo family. It may be that scientific study would reveal connections between Ijaw and other members of the Niger Congo family through these apparent abberations.

The similarity of language in Talbot's identification of the Ijaw seems to be accepted by all scholars who have studied Delta languages.[19] We may now look at the society and customs of the Ijaw through the particular community of Brass or Nembe, which stands as a bridge between the western Ijaw and the more sophisticated subgroups to the east.

2

SOCIAL AND POLITICAL ORGANIZATION

HOUSE RULE

In their dealings with the early white traders, the effectiveness of the coastal communities was due in large measure to the cohesiveness of their social organization. The basis of this organization was the House (*Wari*). What has come to be called House Rule would appear to be of ancient origin, but the system may very well have attained its highest development during the nineteenth century. European observers, perhaps because of their preoccupation with trade, have tended to view the Houses as trading organizations. Tradition and what still remains of the ancient system, however, proves that House Rule was the basis of the entire social, political, and economic organization of the peoples of the Nigerian Delta coastlands.

De Cardi's Observation

Count C. N. de Cardi,[1] a veteran West Coaster, has given a comprehensive account of the social system of the Nembe people as he observed it in the last decades of the nineteenth century. De Cardi distinguished several grades or classes. First came the kings, and second the chiefs and their sons, this last a class that had amassed wealth by trade.

As a third class de Cardi had much to say about persons he termed "Winnaboes." This grade was made up of head slaves or favorite

11

slaves who had the distinction of carrying the chiefs' snuff boxes (*akoto*). They rose to wealth and influence by taking their masters' palm oil down for sale to the white traders. If a Winnabo was tactful in his dealings, the white trader would normally make him a present in cloth according to the number of puncheons supplied. The Winnabo would then hand these collections to his "mother—the woman who had taken care of him from the time he arrived in Brass. When this accumulated property got up to an amount sufficient to buy thirty gallons of palm oil (*pulo angba*), the Winnabo then arranged to invest it in his master's trade. If he had been rendering the master faithful service, or if his "mother" was influential, the terms of this trade arrangement were easy. The Winnabo obtained his share of palm produce from the up-country markets and, selling it to the white man, gradually became well-to-do. He might even come to settle his master's debts with the white traders or succeed his master as a chief. But as long as the master was alive, the Winnabo was subject to his absolute authority.

De Cardi characterizes the fourth class as "Egboboes" (derived from Igbobo: a person from the Ibo country, a slave) or an "absolute lower rank of slaves." These were employed in the oil trade canoes and gigs of the chiefs. They also performed all the meaner and harder work in the towns—any menial jobs that were not performed by the women slaves. According to de Cardi, they were given no more than one good meal a day, and when trade was less brisk they may have been completely neglected. (This class accordingly was the worst hit during the stoppage of trade on the Brass River occasioned by the Royal Niger Company's fiscal policies.) A member of the class had little opportunity to rise in the social scale unless he were employed by a white trader as cabin boy and so learned English and the white man's ways.

De Cardi gives an interesting definition of a House.

A tribe is composed of a king and a number of chiefs. Each chief has a number of petty chiefs under him. Perhaps a better definition for the latter would be, a number of men who own a few slaves and a few canoes of their own, and do an independent trade with the white men, but who pay to their chiefs a tribute of from 20 to 25 percent on their trade with the white man. In many cases the white man stops this tribute from the petty chiefs and holds it on behalf of the chiefs. This collection of petty chiefs with their chief forms what in coast parlance is denominated a House.[2]

The House may reside in a particular quarter of the capital city, Nembe, which it owns in common. The chief or his petty chiefs may own parts of smaller towns or farms, settlements, or fishing villages. All these constitute the communal property of the House. When a petty chief dies, the head chief may seize whatever property was left; it was necessary, however, to the dignity and prestige of the chief to have many subordinate chiefs, and a successor was normally appointed. De Cardi gives evidence of a well-known fact — the strength of custom and public opinion. A particular chief may succeed in overriding them for a time, but one of his successors is bound to pay for his sins in the end.

De Cardi's account reveals a remarkable insight into the House system in the Nembe area. His technique of grading, however, is artificial and gives a wrong impression of society. The class he terms "Winnabo" cannot be traced to any known local word. His other grade or class, "Egboboes," is actually a general term for slaves. The original word for slave is "omonibo." But because most slaves were obtained from the Ibo country, the term "Igbobo," meaning "Iboman," became synonymous with slave. De Cardi thus merely applies the general term to a particular rank of slaves.

De Cardi further defines a House as a "collection of petty chiefs with their chiefs." This highlights an important element of the system — an element tending to keep it democractic. The head of the House (waridab'ō — wari: house; dab'ō: person at the head) or chief (alab'ō) has constantly to seek the cooperation of the heads of families (furoteb'ebō — furo: family). (See Note on Transliteration for diacritic marks.) It is these family or household heads whom de Cardi calls "petty chiefs." The House has on this score been described as a federation of families.

Native House Rule Proclamation and Ordinances

In 1900 Sir Ralph Moore became the high commissioner of the Protectorate of Southern Nigeria. The revenues of the new administration were geared to the trade of the territory. This trade in turn was still very much under the control of the chiefs and middlemen of the Delta city-states. Moreover, the new high commissioner had the job of pacifying the interior districts of his territory before he could begin to govern it. The peoples of the coastal states were yet the only groups that could be said to have been brought under British colonial authority. It was under such circumstances that the Native House Rule Proclamation, 1901, came into being.

In 1901 Sir Ralph Moore drafted his Slave Dealing Proclamation. All the chiefs and House heads he consulted at Bonny, Opobo, Degema, and Brass, in fear that their Houses would break up, were united in their opposition to the new rule. To avert this, to placate the chiefs, and to prevent a total stoppage of trade, it was decided to issue the Native House Rule Proclamation, 1901.[3] The Native House Rule Proclamation was indeed conceived of as a corollary to the Slave Dealing Proclamation, 1901. It was intended to abolish both the practice and the status of slavery and at the same time to convert the slaves within the coastal communities into full House members and responsible citizens.

The proclamation defined House as follows:

"House" means a group of persons subject by Native Law and Custom to the control, authority, and rule of a chief, known as a Head of House.

The proclamation imposed on any insubordinate member of a House a maximum fine of £50, one year's imprisonment, or both. Any vagrant House member could also be arrested and imprisoned for a maximum period of one year. Even employers were liable to a fine (£50) and/or imprisonment (one year) if they failed to seek the permission of the House head before engaging a House member.

For the protection of the House member, it was laid down that a House head who neglected to perform his duties under native law and custom toward House members was to be fined up to £50 or imprisoned for a year. Every action under the proclamation was further to pass through a district commissioner.

As the government became more firmly established, the need to please the chiefs became less and less important. In 1912 the Native House Rule (Amendment) Ordinance allowed a House member to buy himself off. It was the district commissioner and not the House head who was to fix the amount, which was in no case to exceed £50, or £15 for "persons of the labouring class or canoe boys." Such a member was to lose all privileges of membership and claims to communal rights and property of the House, but was "to retain and remove all his own personal property."

Other amendments in 1913 restricted the application of the ordinance to Calabar, Bonny, Opobo, Degema, Brass, Warri, and Sapele.

There had been mistaken applications "to the up-country districts where Houses are unknown." Order No. 19 of the 1913 amendment removed the trial of causes under the Native House Rule Ordinance from the native courts. The House, too, was redefined:

"House" means a number of persons grouped together for the purposes of trade and subject by native law and custom to the control, authority, and rule of a chief known as the Head of the house.

Official interpretation of House Rule was dominated after this by the misconception that Houses were constituted solely "for the purposes of trade," and that a House could be divided into an oppressed slave class and an exploiting free minority. It was with this understanding that Lord Lugard suggested the setting up of "trading corporations" in place of the Houses when it was proposed to repeal the House Rule Proclamation and Ordinances.[4] And when it was finally decided simply to repeal the Ordinance, effective January 1, 1915, the Anti-Slavery and Aborigines Protection Society, London, passed a resolution congratulating the Secretary of State for the Colonies and Lugard for finally destroying the "indigenous forms of slave-owning" in Nigeria.

Internal Evidence

Before the Native House Rule Proclamation and Ordinances were repealed, the chiefs from the Itsekiri, Urhobo, Brass, Degema, Okrika, Bonny, Opobo, and Calabar areas were asked their views. The matter was presented in a way to suggest that the repeal of these ordinances would mean the abolition of Houses. Accordingly, the result was a series of alarmed petitions from these chiefs, who knew that House Rule had not been established by the proclamation and the ordinances but had been the basis of the social organization of their society for decades before then. These petitions also reveal the nature and internal working of the House system.[5]

Chiefs Dore Numa and Nana of Itsekiri asserted that if repeal was to mean the abolition of House Rule, it would mean their "final ruin." Compensation would be no good because House heads would simply "eat" it and then "sit down and die." It would mean the ruin not only of House heads but also of trade, of the spirit of mutual help, and of service to elders and the infirm. Vagrancy and crime would increase; some members, however, would be bound after a time to return to their Houses when they found conditions difficult. The Brass chiefs made the following points in their petition.

1. The House Rule measures were passed after the abolition of slavery in 1901, and, as there has been no contravention of the Slavery Proclamation, there was no point in repealing House Rule.

2. There was already provision in native law and custom for a member to contract out of a House on the condition that (a) he forfeit all personal property and (b) pay a redemption fee equal in amount to the original purchase sum.

3. The House is a corporate and mutual organization in which every individual has a right to succeed to the headship.

4. It would be unjust for House heads to be deserted in their old age by members who had in the first place been nurtured by them.

The chiefs of Nembe never really gave up the struggle against the repeal of the House Rule Ordinances. For some years after 1915 all joint addresses or petitions to the government contained an appeal to do something to strengthen the authority of the House heads. A petition[6] of August 1920 is of special interest because a memorandum, "Native Laws and Customs Respecting Community," was attached explaining the nature of the House system. The memorandum is given in full:

1. In Brass the term House, which today is substituted with the name community, implies a body of people comprising a notable man and the progeny of three branches of his people, viz: — his children, his relatives, and his domestics. The said noble man [is] the Head of the Community, otherwise called the Chief, and the three branches of people and their children being the members.

2. The acquirements or income or earnings of every member of the Community belongs to the whole Community, and are under the control of the Head of the Community.

3. When the original Head of the Community dies, the cleverest and most ambitious amongst the members is elected to take the Headship.

4. The members of the Community are at liberty to live various and separate places, though they are bound to observe the laws, and to carry out the duties, of their Community wherever they reside.

5. When a member of a Community dies, his corpse is taken from his station to the headquarters and is buried there by the head of his Community. The burial expenses being subscribed and undergone by all the

members of the deceased's Community. The same is done in the case
of the Head of the Community when he dies.

6. (a) If any member of the Community owe a heavy debt, the whole
Community subscribes for the payment of it.

(b) If a great case crops up against the Head or any member of the
Community, the whole Community raises a subscription to defray the expenditure thereof, as well as [to] assist in pulling
over to any distance (as the case may be) and witness the settlement of such case. In short, the Head of the Community cares
and helps all the members of his Community both male and
female, in sickness, in poverty, in bad debts, in puerperal
and funeral matters, and when involved in great cases.

7. If any Government authority as the Resident, or Governor, etc.,
require the Head or Chief to appear before him in a distant place to
discuss matters, the Head is pulled and brought over by the young members of the Community, and these are called the Gig boys who are required to live near the Head of the Community.

8. If a work is set by a Government Official for the Chiefs to do in
the town, or if there be any work of the Communities, the members
of the Communities are bound to do it at the command of the Heads of
the Communities.

9. Besides the gig boys mentioned above, the men in every Community
are arranged into four classes (i) the Head, (ii) subhead, (iii) the primary members and (iv) the ordinary members.

10. The men of the preceding three classes in the Community trade
and work independently towards the welfare and up-keeping of the
Community; those of the second and third classes supporting the Head
by giving him trade tax; and the men of the fourth class, while being
independent and carrying on their personal trades too, assist and support
the Community by trading for the Head or Chief. In short, all the men
in the Community are expected to work for the existence of the Community. At the same time all the men of the latter three classes are subject to promotion.

11. Besides other assistances, the Heads of Communities are bound
to give every member of their Communities goods and money to trade
for themselves.

12. In foreign countries, where they live on farming, the members of
Communities used to work on the farms of the Heads of their Communities, and used also to contribute yams, etc., for their Heads to live on. But
in this part here where we have no large lands for farming as in other
places, we live on trade: hence some members of the Community help
the Head by trading for him at times.

13. If any of the female members of a Community is to be married by a man, her parents are first consulted and then by their approval, the consent of the Head of her Community is unavoidably obtained by the intending husband for, according to our native custom, a marriage is void since the intending husband has not obtained due consent or approval from the Head of the Community to which his intended wife belongs.

14. When a member of a Community refuses to obey the Head against the general laws and orders of the Community, such member is imposed to necessary fine.

15. If a member of a Community claims to leave his or her Community entirely, he or she is at liberty to do so, but on condition that he or she leaves all his or her substance and belongings for the Community [that] he or she had been a member of, for he or she had doubtless gained them from that Community. The foregoing are the customs and laws of our country whereby we have hitherto ruled and supported our Communities and country, without which laws and customs, there would have been no Community, no trade, and eventually no country. Therefore we humbly claim that Your Excellency may cause the Communities to be recognized as formerly.

Memoranda submitted by the other Delta chiefs show that the House Rule system was similarly organized in all these areas. The Itsekiri definition of "member of House" had the same threefold division:

1. Persons received by purchase or pawn;
2. Children born into the House by such persons; and
3. All other ordinary members.

It may be added that House membership can also be increased by the acceptance of political refugees, that is, persons who seek protection from the oppression of other Houses or towns. The Itsekiri procedure for persons wishing to withdraw from House membership was also similar to the Nembe custom. A person who was originally pawned regained freedom on payment of a sum equal to the original debt. A former slave had to repay a sum double the original purchase fee of himself or parent. In each case all property acquired during the period of membership was to be given up.

It becomes clear that the House was far from being primarily a commercial corporation. Equally, it was not primarily a form of slave owning. It was rather an association for maintaining law and order in society — a form of social security and insurance. An aspect of the system that is better recognized by the people is the military significance of the organization. A House is thus sometimes referred to as a War Canoe House — meaning a House that has the capacity to man a war canoe in defense of the city-state. A House did not, in fact, become fully recognized as such until it demonstrated this mili-tary or naval capacity.

During a national war, therefore, each full-fledged House was required to equip at least one war canoe. The minimum number of fighting men necessary for this purpose was thirty; this figure was accordingly taken as the lower limit of qualification for recognition. There were many Houses capable of launching several war canoes. In an assessment report of 1929, for example, Captain J. N. Hill gave the following numbers of taxable males in a few of the Houses.

Ogbolomabiri				Bassambiri			
Ockiya	237	Gam Dede	45	Ewowari	97	Ogbu	55
Ogbari	52	Igbeta	187	Elema	53	Kari	108
Oruwari	57	Yekorogha	96	Bugo	72	Egbelu	50
Yemainain	66	Koko	104	Tamono	72	Arisimo	40
Amain	123	Amangi	29	Epemu	43	Ebifa	33
(Kien)	60			Pegi	96		

SOME RECENT HOUSES

The repeal of the House Rule Ordinance did not mean the death of House Rule: there was no exodus from the Houses. The most serious effect, however, was the weakening of the authority of the heads of Houses. But even here the ultimate causes may be traced to changes in economic circumstances and to the impact of Western ways. The House system continues to be a vital social force and has important effects, and sometimes unfortunate ones in local politics.

Rather than diminishing, veneration for the spirits of the ancestors and original founders of Houses increased. Mausoleums and memori-als (*Okpu*) have been erected to most of the prominent ancient chiefs. Until a few years ago these memorials or shrines were the most solid and beautiful buildings in the towns.

The establishment of native administration gave the House heads something to do. They were appointed to the councils and courts and entrusted with the collection of taxes from their House members. This, of course, led to suits against members who refused to recognize the authority of certain House heads. But the most eloquent sign of the vitality of the House Rule system is the fact that new and vigorous Houses have actually sprung up in comparatively recent times.

Alagoa House. The Alagoa House is a part of and an off-shoot of the Amain-Kien House, which is now known as the Amain-Kien-Alagoa House. The eldest branch of this trinity is obviously Amain — the founder of the House group being King Boy Amain, son and successor of King Forday Kulo (and the man who rescued the Lander Brothers from Aboh in 1830). Kien, the other partner, succeeded Amain as amanyanabo (king).

After Kien, the Amain-Kien House was headed by Edmund Natebo (Kien branch) and Joseph Alagoa. Chief Joseph Alagoa was a grandson of King Boy Amain, his mother Yeh being the king's daughter. His father was Chief Elema of Bassambiri. Oral history says he was recalled from Okpoma to be head of his grandfather's House "when Ockiya was King" (which indicates a date prior to 1879 and after 1863). Edmund Natebo died in 1904, to be succeeded by Joe Natebo in the headship of the Kien House. Both Chief Joseph Alagoa and Joe Natebo died in July 1934.

The members of the Amain-Kien House met to elect new heads in November 1935. It would normally only have been necessary to elect a head for the Amain House and another for the Kien House together with their supporters and elders. This could not be in this case. Chief Joseph Alagoa had been a great chief, had ruled the combined House for so long, acquired so many personal followers, and made such a name both with the white man and with the people that his name could not possibly be dropped. Moreover, the government even before the old chief's death had allowed his son Edward Alagoa to sit on his behalf in the native court in 1932, as "representing the Head of the Alagoa House." [7] It was accordingly agreed to elect Edward Alagoa head of the new Alagoa House as a memorial to his father's name. The other heads were Clement Mendie Kien (Kien House) and Olukutu Amain (Amain House and senior head of the combined Amain-Kien-Alagoa House). The veneration the people had for Chief Joseph Alagoa was such that the government subsidy formerly paid to him as head of the combined House was passed on to his son.

Edward Alagoa died in March 1938 and was succeeded by Moses O. Alagoa as head of the Alagoa House on November 29, 1939. He was formally introduced to the chiefs of Nembe, according to custom, on December 1, 1939, and to the assistant district officer of Brass on December 4.[8] The current head of the Alagoa House is Chief the Hon. Francis O. Joseph Alagoa, Mingi X, Amanyanabo of Nembe.

I was present on the occasion of the election of Francis O. J. Alagoa as head of his father's house. Chief Olukutu had also died and there was need to appoint heads for both the Alagoa and Amain Houses. Chief Clement Mendie Kien presided. Speeches were made by the chairman and several elders on internal House affairs. Aspirants to nomination made speeches criticizing the conduct of House affairs in the past. Former holders of places spoke either in self-defence or declared their readiness to retire, if so required. The gathering of the whole Amain-Kien-Alagoa House then split into groups to suggest possible candidates for election. The groups consisted of elders and family heads (or subchiefs), a middle-age group, the young men, and the women. Each group conferred together and frankly discussed the leaders. The general time for speeches had, of course, already disclosed who the likely favorites were. When the Chairman called the meeting together, a spokesman of each group gave the names of the persons they wished to be head and deputy head of each of the three Houses. The result was that Chief Clement Mendie Kien was made the senior head of the combined House and became head of Amain House, Regould Debo was named head of Kien House, and Francis O. J. Alagoa head of Alagoa House.

The meeting was brought to a close by the new chiefs making speeches.[9] They were later shown to the chiefs and the town in a ceremony of investment at the town square.

Febo House. A dispute arose in 1938 about the existence of the Febo House. In that year the members of the House elected Clement Otiotio to be head of the Febo House. The amanyanabo of Bassambiri, Chief Ben Warri, gave his blessing to the proceedings. Chief Berema Duguruyai, head of Duguruyai House, objected to the new head of Febo House having a seat in the Native Administration Council on the grounds (1) that Febo was a part of Duguruyai House; and (2) that the approval given by the amanyanabo of Bassambiri constituted an interference in the internal affairs of the Duguruyai House.

The assistant district officer, who was petitioned on the matter, concluded that there had indeed been a separate Febo House in the past. The House declined after the death of its founder and became merged with the Duguruyai House. Subsequent heads of the Febo House were accordingly appointed on the approval of the head of Duguruyai House. The Febo House, by 1938, had regained its war canoe strength — that is, it had no less than thirty male adults to man a war canoe.

The dispute was settled on September 5, 1938, when the new head of Febo House apologized to the head of Duguruyai House "for trying to break away from the Duguruyai House without the consent of the House Head." Chief Berema Duguruyai on his part accepted the apology and recognized Clement Febo as head of Febo House.[10]

Ayah House. The origin of Ayah House was revealed in a dispute over who was to become amanyanabo of Ewoama in 1938. Ayah was apparently a "money chief" of Mein's House in Bassambiri. He had a difference with Mein and was forced to flee. He went first to Twon, where he was sheltered by a friend, Boutebe. He realized later that Twon was too open to Mein's influence and sought greater security in Okpoma. Orukare was the amanyanabo of Okpoma. Other prominent House heads included Eseni, Pegiyai, and Aguma. The more important chiefs in Okpoma were also priests of the town's gods. Orukare was associated with Osuan or Odu, Pegiyai with Mina, and Aguma with Okuru. When Ayah arrived in Okpoma, he touched the shrine of Mina and was accordingly proclaimed a devotee of that god and a member of Pegiyai House, and entitled to the protection of that House.

Ayah in time became regent in succession to Orukare and priest of Mina. He later followed the Pegiyai House to Ewoama when that House fought a civil war with the Orukare House. Digiboerigha, who led the faction to found Ewoama, was a grandson of Pegiyai and became the first amanyanabo. He was succeeded by Thomas Abayeh, who died on November 15, 1914. Chief Iyabi succeeded to the control of the House and town in the following year. The history of Ewoama, which so far had been the history of a single united war canoe House, ends from this time on. A faction apparently wished Iyabi to adopt the name Abayeh. This was refused. A split resulted, which has since made it impossible for Ewoama to select an amanyanabo. The town has been split into the two houses of Pegiyai and Ayah.

ORIGINS OF HOUSES

These examples show something of the complexities of the internal organization of Houses. There is little doubt that close investigation of the origin and development of each House in the Nembe Clan would reveal more of the origins of the people than many another procedure. The fact is that all the people of Nembe stock are attached to one House or the other and that individuals and towns are in this way related by blood. The rival quarters of Nembe — Bassambiri and Ogbolomabiri — are, for example, known to have sprung from the two cousins Ogbodo and Mingi from whom the Houses of each quarter grew. All the Houses in Ogbolomabiri have thus been traced to the sons and daughters of Mingi — King Forday Kulo having pride of place as producing the greatest number of sons and grandsons who were able to build Houses around them.[11] Mingi's son and successor as amanyanabo, Ikata, was the ancestor of Oruwari and of the Oruwari House. Chief Omo was another son of Mingi around whom Ockiya and Berena Houses developed. King Kulo is the connecting link between a whole series of Houses — Amain, Kien, Iboama, Igbeta, Bugo, John, Egebe, Yekorogha, and others. Mingi's daughters Ingo and Ine account for the Koko and Yemainain Houses. The Ogbari House is descended from Chief Ogbari, son of the first Mingi.

An unfortunate grouping of the Houses into two camps occurs in Ogbolomabiri at times of stress. Those Houses directly descended from King Kulo call themselves the Kulo House. The others group themselves into a Mingi House.

In conclusion, a peculiar social effect of the House system may be noted. The desire to increase and strengthen Houses, together with the system of matrilineal succession, has had unfortunate results. A child grew up into the House of its mother, and women were accordingly looked upon with favor for their sons and daughters would increase House membership. It was apparently for this reason too that parents and House heads did not practice the custom of requiring large dowries. Female members of Houses could and were encouraged to marry outside and to bring in their children. Male members, on the other hand, had two ways of avoiding the misfortune of bearing children for other Houses. They could take wives from their own Houses. Better still, they could marry women from outside the Nembe area with "big dowry." ("Big dowry" meant the payment of a higher amount of bride-wealth than was customary in Nembe — an amount often normal for the patrilineal societies from which the women were obtained.) This was what the kings and more powerful chiefs did to ensure that their children remained in their Houses to succeed them. The custom of matrilineal succession is now under attack. It has been found that uncles take little interest in the education of there sisters' children. Fathers also considered themselves free of all responsibility for their children — children who would, in any case, go to their mothers' Houses.

In sum, House Rule is an ancient system the Nembe people shared with Itsekiri, Kalabari, Okrika, Bonny, and Efik. It was developed during the turbulent days before the institution of "white" government. It was an organization which measured the importance of each unit by the number of breeding females in it, by the wealth of its members, and by the fighting and working males it could muster. It was a democratic organization in which the head or chief had to consult with the family heads or subchiefs, all of whom were elected to office by the whole body of House members. Because the size, importance, and strength of the House had to be kept up, its women were not to marry into another House; its men were encouraged to marry by big dowry by marrying outside the clan; and slaves were not mistreated but were rather encouraged to develop initiative, acquire wealth, and contribute to the well being of the House.

Government withdrawal of support did not kill the Houses, but it has progressively weakened their cohesiveness. House heads can no longer fulfill their duties under the system as the members no longer work for them or for the Houses. It is here that the economic aspect of the system becomes most important. The real enemy of the system is the displacement of a communal organization by the rise of individualism fostered by the new economic and social conditions.

THE MONARCHY

Nembe, like the other city-states in the eastern Delta, was a monarchy. The king or amanyanabo had powers which may be described as constitutional or customary rather than absolute. He was the first among the chiefs of the clan, and each chief, after appointment by members of his House, had to obtain the king's commission in a public ceremony of investiture at the public square (*opupolotiri*). The chief then became a member of the king's council.

The king was himself appointed on the unanimous decision of the chiefs of the metropolis. And the ceremony of coronation included the curious act of a senior chief striking the new amanyanabo lightly on the head. This apparently signified that the ruler had on the day of his coronation endured the last act of indignity or humiliation at the hands of his subjects. He was thenceforward raised above all his subjects, but was constrained to consult with his chiefs and the high priest in matters like the declaration of war. The limit and extent of the king's prerogative, however, were determined in practice by the influence and character of the man chosen to rule.

Tact and good performance stood a king in good stead, for in addition to the chiefs in the metropolis he had to see to the lesser amanyanabo of the subordinate towns.

In the very early days the king was also high priest and was called, not amanyanabo, but oboluma pere, olodiama pere, or onyoma pere.[12] But even in those days there was a tribunal or final court of appeal known as Ibidi and said to have been held at a place in Olodiama. It was held in secret and the guilty never got anything less than the death sentence or exile.

All laws, proclamations, and enactments were made in the king's name. He did not judge save in council with his chiefs. The judicial system, however, was such that it allowed the king to exercise a strong influence. Offenses against the king's person were treated with greater severity than when they were committed against commoners. Adultery, for example, was normally viewed as a grave offence, but it became doubly so if committed with one of the king's wives. Adulterer and adulteress were bound together and drowned in a creek known as Kikoliyai.[13]

LEADERSHIP IN WAR [14]

The traditional histories stress the martial aspects of the activities of kings and the people. This is understandable as the national god, Ogidiga, was, like Jehovah, a god of hosts.

The high priest was intimately concerned with the declaration of war and with the ceremonies at the close of it. The god was consulted through him before war could be declared, and the sacrifice of captives had to be carried out under his advice and direction.

The skulls of sacrificed captives were preserved as trophies in an altar — *egbesu*. Each was painted with camwood on one side and chalk on the other. A particular sword kept in this grove or altar — *Isene Ogidi* [15] — was obviously related to the god Ogidiga and was greatly reverenced. It was not to be spoken of lightly or in jest and was useful as an instrument of justice, for no one could swear by it and speak falsely.

The king was the key figure in the prosecution of any war. After the customary consultations with his chiefs and the priest, the declaration of war or peace was done in the king's name. He was also commander-in-chief and was expected to lead the attack in person. He could not delegate this duty: such action would be tantamount to abdicating his position. Each of his chiefs would command, in person, one or more war canoes manned by members of their respective Houses. The various villages would come in and serve under House heads in Nembe or under the banner of local House heads or of their amanyanabo.

The chiefs and the amanyanabo of the allied towns could wage their own private wars, but only with the permission of the amanyanabo of Nembe. Thus, when Ockiya (before he became Mingi VII) wanted to go to Amassoma to prosecute a case of three of his brothers seized for a debt, he had to obtain King Kien's permission. The king gave him a barrel of rum, as well as two men to assist him, who were to report back. Ockiya succeeded in arranging a peaceful settlement. During his own reign Ockiya enforced this convention of peaceful settlement on the people of Okpoma who had kidnapped and killed nine men from the Ogbia town of Okpokiri without permission — and against the ruling of King Kien that no hostile action should be taken against Okpokiri. A fine was imposed on Okpoma, and it was enforced by seizing some of its men as hostages.

REGALIA, STATE PROPERTY

A new king of Nembe was not supplied with a palace. He was expected to use his office and the services of his subjects to acquire for himself a place worthy of his position. The personal initiative of the king was important and what he was able to acquire for the crown went to improve the position of his successor. By his dynamism or power he might win new privileges from the white traders on the river or new lands from neighboring states. Such rights did not belong to the king's House and family but to the monarchy and the state. It was thus that the insignia of royalty and the material attributes to awe and majesty increased for the amanyanabo of Nembe through the ages.

There were some items of royal property that were purchased at each coronation with money raised by public subscription. Thus, at the coronation of Anthony Ockiya in 1926, a royal umbrella, a gold ring, two scepters, crowns, robes, flags, and other personal adornments were supplied. The amanyanabo was also furnished with part of a new house. Some of these items had to be provided at each coronation because they often had to be buried with the ruler at his death, or were lost or destroyed from use. However, other property was handed down from relative antiquity.[16]

Many of the emblems of royalty can be traced to King Kulo but began to be most effectively used from the reign of his dynamic son King Boy Amain. The *ikirigo* or talking drum for summoning people to meetings was brought from Bonny by King Boy Amain and presented to his father King Forday Kulo. Since then only the king has been entitled to use it.

The ringing of a bell—especially in a royal canoe on the Brass River—has also come to be a royal privilege. This too would appear to have begun from Kulo's reign. A first set of seven bells was brought from Bonny, one of which was presented to Duguruyai of Bassambiri. The right of ringing it on the river, however, remained with the ruler of Ogbolomabiri. The royal bell was handed down from Kulo to his son Amain, to Kien, and down to Constantine Ockiya and Frederick Koko. During the "Akassa Raid" (1895) organized by King Koko, a new bell was won. Chief Felix Amabebe Smoke is said to have taken a bell from the ship "Nupe" at Akassa and to have handed it over to Koko at the distribution of the booty. This may have been the bell given to Anthony Ockiya, or the one given to Anthony may have been the original Kulo bell.

The use of royal umbrellas was certainly an established custom when the Landers visited Nembe in 1830 during the reign of King Kulo.[17] It is clear that these umbrellas were replaced as they grew old or were destroyed. But any that remained intact at the close of a reign were passed on to the successor. Like the bell, only the king could use the umbrella on the river in a ceremonial manner.

Three elephant tusks have been preserved. They were all pre-

sented to rulers by friendly supercargoes on the Brass River. The first
was a present to King Boy Amain and inscribed as follows:

To King Boy of the Brass country — Ammi of the town Obullama — son
and successor to the Great King Forday. This is presented as a memorial
of the honor and integrity universally displayed by him in his transactions with the donor A.D. 1846.

The other two were presents to King Kien (1846–1863) and King
Ockiya (1863–1879), and were both in the possession of King Anthony Ockiya (1926–1936). King Ockiya's ivory had been presented
by a Captain Pearman.

It was also the prerogative of the king to take charge of all river
courses and public lands throughout the Nembe area. Accordingly,
the lists of property handed to new rulers always included the names
of various river inlets, fishing flats, bushes, and building sites. In
the time of the earlier kings, sole authority was vested in the ruler
to authorize fishing in rivers or flats or settlement in unoccupied
bushes or mangroves. When European traders arrived, therefore, it
was the kings of Nembe who negotiated terms. By the same token,
comey dues and, later, rents were paid to the kings and to no others.

The comey collected from the supercargoes trading at Twon, and
later the rent from the consular government, in time became one of
the main sources of royal revenue. Its collection became so important
that in 1889 King Koko had to obtain a refund of rents paid to a
regent before his accession. From the reign of King Anthony Ockiya,
however, the rents have been shared among all the chiefs.[18]

There is a herd of royal cattle at Nembe said to date from as early
as the reign of Ogio, the fifth king of Nembe. He had collected two
cows as presents from the king of Saka when he married the Saka
princess, Kalaere. These became the nucleus of a herd.

The origin of the royal flags is not clear. A union jack and bell,
or *igbema*, flag were flown by a king. The union jack was probably
used as a sign of friendship for the British consul and the British
sovereign.

On the death of a king, the head of the king's House took custody
of all royal property until a new ruler was appointed. But during the
long period of interregnum at the beginning of this century, unsuccessful attempts were made by individuals to appropriate some state
property for themselves or for their Houses.

DUAL MONARCHY — OGBOLOMABIRI AND BASSAMBIRI

The two principal quarters of the metropolis have a king each and a history of rivalry. A number of cases submitted to independent arbitration have established, however, that the Mingi line at Ogbolomabiri was sovereign.

The first incident leading to arbitration came in January 1927 when Albert Oguara, amanyanabo of Bassambiri, declared his intention to ring a bell on the river and to use a ceremonial umbrella. The controversy was continued by Chief Ben Warri, Oguara's successor in 1928; and Captain Hill, on April 5, 1929, had to decide in favour of Anthony Ockiya, amanyanabo of Ogbolomabiri, in respect to "(1) Ringing the bell on the River; (2) Carrying the Amanyanabo umbrella on the river."[19]

In attempting to carry out these ceremonial symbols of sovereignty, the amanyanabo of Bassambiri had argued that he was in all respects equal to his neighbour. Captain Hill rightly concluded that Ogbolomabiri was "the eldest and the original headquarters of Nembe," and that the attempt to carry out the ceremonies was a maneuver by the radical elements in Bassambiri to take advantage of a long interregnum in Ogbolomabiri.

A full-scale government commission[20] in 1959 came to basically the same conclusions as Hill had in 1929. The sole commissioner, Mr. Ukelonu, after studying the traditions of the civil war that led to the separation of the quarters in the first place,[21] decided that sovereignty had then permanently passed to the Mingi line.

A KING'S BURIAL

Widespread and prolonged lamentation was made at the death of a king.[22] The body, decked in costly raiment and jewelry, lay in state for three days, having been treated with aromatic substances and thus enabling subjects from all corners of the kingdom to attend the ceremonies. The high priest took a large share in conducting affairs. All Houses in Nembe exerted themselves to show their respect to the late king: dances were staged and guns were fired by day and by night. Tepowa gives the dimensions of the grave as twenty-five feet by thirty feet and from twelve feet to sixteen feet deep. It was dug in the king's house or compound and would afterward be kept scrupulously clean by members of his household. It later became a spot to be visited by devoted friends and relatives. The coffin itself was lined with silks, velvets, and corals. According to Tepowa, the last item signified royalty — as in Benin.

A war dance — *peri toi* — was performed as part of the ceremonies following the death of a king or high priest.[23] The dance, or play, was a representation of the act of killing a war captive at the place of sacrifice by cutting off the victim's head. It was accordingly performed by a fraternity of persons who had actually cut off the heads of men they had captured in war. These men were accorded high honor in society and were distinguished by the fact that they drank with their left hands and, with each other, shook hands with the left. The play was also performed when one of their number died. They would arrive on the field with chalked arms and with a white eagle's feather in their cap, armed with matchets. They were led out to the arena by the eldest son or nearest relative of the deceased and, as the war drums struck up, they gesticulated furiously and enacted the acts of war and of dispatching the enemy. The appropriate war calls would be made.

The ceremony of offering wine to the spirits of previous kings — *kamo* — had also to be performed by the eldest son or nearest relative. This was done at the public square round which stood the vaults or memorial halls (*okpu*) of past kings. The performer held two wine glasses filled with wine; as the spirit moved him and the drums beat, he danced round, spilling wine at the doors of each of the *okpu*. The spilling of wine was done involuntarily, for the hands of the performer would be possessed and tremble. He moved to a different *okpu* as the drums beat out the title of each dead hero-king. The glasses were refilled from time to time, and new glasses were supplied as old ones were broken.

De Cardi has left an account of the burial of King Kien of Ogbolomabiri and King Arisimo of Bassambiri.[24] The ceremony was identical for both rulers. He estimates the grave at fourteen by twelve feet and about eight feet deep, dug on a piece of ground near but not inside the King's house. A table spread with liquors and other delicacies was laid at a chamber of the grave, and over this chamber were laid stout beams. The head of the king faced this way. The grave was then covered over, with the exception of a small hole down which offerings of wine would be poured in later days. Part of the earth dug out of the grave was used to make the walls of a hut that was built over the grave.

The corpse was allowed to remain in state for only two days; the preservatives used could not permit of the longer period of mourning. The body was dressed in "most expensive robes, having round the neck several necklaces of valuable coral." His chiefs added their own strings as they arrived for the ceremony. The European supercargoes on the Brass River were also expected to contribute and often tried to outdo each other in the value and quantity of their presents. The standard contribution was "a cask of beef, a barrel of rum, a hundred weight of ship's biscuits, and from twenty to thirty pieces of cloth."

De Cardi confirms the tradition of gun-firing. This was done during the whole period of lying in state and as long after as the successor could afford. Cannons were used for the public firing, but individuals shot "the ordinary trade gun." It is interesting to note that de Cardi saw no form of human sacrifice in any of the two burials he observed:

Towards ten o'clock of the second night after death the King was placed in a very open-work wicker casket, and carried shoulder high round the town, and then finally deposited in his grave. I and another European concealed ourselves near the grave, and carefully watched all night to see if they sacrificed any slaves on the King's grave, or put any poor creatures down into the graves to die a lingering death; but we saw nothing of this done. . . .

The Reverend Thomas Johnson, who was missionary at Twon when Arisimo died on July 20, 1870, also came down to Bassambiri. His estimate for the size of the grave agrees with de Cardi's: "about 12 feet long and 8 feet broad." According to Johnson, there was feasting instead of mourning and about a thousand pounds worth of goods were buried with the king.[25]

Tepowa also gives a description of the burial of King Frederick William Koko (died February 25, 1898) that sounds like an eyewitness account or one taken from an eyewitness.[26] The body lay in state for three days, during which time people came from all parts of the outlying country. Guns and cannons were shot by all chiefs and village headmen. His children were clad in the late king's clothes and went round the town in a solemn procession. "The best beloved son of the deceased by his first wife was borne aloft by four men, leading the procession — he being regarded as the late King's representative." The grave was three-feet square, with a square depth of twelve feet, neatly cemented at the bottom, and closely sealed with boards at the top. It was decorated with "rich silks" and packed with the most valuable property of the dead king. The inside of the coffin itself was "lined with silk and covered outside with the rich velvet stuff contributed by the chiefs." On the seventh day after burial one of the sons was led to the waterside (*opupogu*) and shouted the king's name. He then ran quickly home. This marked the end of the ceremony and was a signal that those who wished could return home and resume their several occupations; but until the ceremony was thus announced to be over, no work was permitted. The widows and other relatives of the late king, however, had a further period of six months to mourn their loss, confined within doors.

The social and political organization of Nembe shows certain factors that may be reasonably characterized as democratic or democratizing. The chief or House head was appointed by vote of all House members. After appointment he could rule harshly, but then individual members could move away to other communities to seek the protection of more powerful and just chiefs. Such disaffection ultimately weakened the chief's standing in the society and acted as a restraint, resulting in the exemplary treatment even of slaves. And the possibility of a revolution could not be completely discounted. These need not be violent: the unpopular chief could simply be deposed. Even when he was too powerful to be directly attacked, retribution could fall on his children and descendants when he was no more.

Position of authority thus carried with it much social prestige and was often attended with much outward show of pomp. At the same time even the office of king — amanyanabo — implied more an office for organizing a consensus on public affairs rather than one of a despotic exercise of authority. He was hedged round with chiefs who could speak as the elected representatives of sections of the community. Tact and a spirit of wise political compromise became important attributes. The king's advantage was that he alone could speak with the united voice of the whole community. The test of his ability was to reconcile the conflicting interests within the state — the interests of House heads and their following; the rival aspirations of the amanyabo of Bassambiri and the towns looking up to him for leadership; and the accession of the outlying groups to decisions made at the center. We will see in the succeeding pages the origins of these institutions and how they have worked through the history of the Brass people.

Dr. Dike divided the city states of the Delta into monarchies — "Bonny (Ibani), New Calabar (Kalabari), and Warri — " and republics, which were "in reality simple trading units with divided political authority as in Old Calabar, Brass, and the Cameroons." [27] This definition of Brass as a republic is not supported by the facts. The system Dr. Dike proceeds to describe for Bonny is in fact similar in all essentials to the monarchical constitution of Brass — the Mingi of Brass being the counterpart of "the Pepples at Bonny and of the Amakiris at New Calabar." [28]

3

LEGENDS OF ORIGIN

All old men are expected to know the story of how Nembe was founded. Knowledge of origins and traditional history is part of the wisdom of old men and women, and they would, at the least, know the details of the origin of their own families and Houses. Chiefs and kings were also men who knew the genealogies of their ancestors far into the remote past and of the wars fought by them. This knowledge would, in fact, have been a factor in their appointment and they took care to surround themselves with experts in history and to hand their knowledge down to sons or to those they wished to succeed them.[1]

The legends given below are therefore commonly told in Nembe to this day. The method adopted is to record the source, as fully as possible, before making an assessment, and an attempt will also be made to throw some light on the interrelations between the various peoples of the Niger Delta as revealed by their legends of origin.

ADEBIYI TEPOWA'S ACCOUNT [2]

Adebiyi Tepowa, who stayed long enough at Nembe to speak and write the language, appears to have had reliable sources for his information. He acknowledged himself "largely indebted to Chief James A. Spiff, also Messrs. David A. Kemmer and John T. Ockiya, late pupil teacher of the C. M. S. Day School, Nembe." [3]

Tepowa begins his story with the arrival in the Nembe area of three strangers, Obolo, Olodia, and Onyo. There is no reference to any peoples living there before their arrival. Obolo, Olodia, and

34

Onyo may have come from Benin or Ijaw, and no reason is given for their immigration to Nembe. Three towns were founded as a result of their immigration, namely, Oboloama, Olodiama, Onyoama (i.e., Obolo's, Olodia's, and Onyo's town). These towns eventually were dispersed by civil war and epidemics.

First, there was a civil war between the peoples of Oboloama and Olodiama. The people of Olodiama, a stronger people, placed fishing stakes opposite Oboloama. This constituted an insult and a challenge. A war resulted in which Olodiama was victorious. The king of Oboloama went to a juju doctor to prepare some weapon against Olodiama. The doctor prepared a medicine with a live tortoise (*ikagi*) — an animal sacred to the people of Olodiama. The king of Oboloama put this tortoise on the water at flood tide and the animal floated onto the shores of Olodiama. There was commotion in the town and people crowded to see the tortoise that had been miraculously brought in by the tide. At the ebb tide it floated back to Oboloama, but at Olodiama all the people who had come out to see the tortoise sickened and died.

The king of Olodiama realized what must have happened. He too went to the juju doctor and offered a larger sum for a more destructive medicine. This time a python (*ekekoru*) was offered. This was put on the water at ebb tide and floated to the beaches at Oboloama. Many people rushed down to see the sacred snake brought down with the tide. It returned to Olodiama at the flood tide, and again those who had seen it at Oboloama sickened and died.

The towns of Oboloama and Olodiama were depleted by this war of knives and juju medicine, but they were not completely destroyed. A civil war occurred at Oboloama occasioned by the distribution of the meat brought in at communal hunting. The cook omitted to leave a share of the soup (*wan fulo*) for one of the most active hunters; this resulted in a feud between the two families which spread to the rest of the town. Oboloama was all but completely destroyed.

The few survivors of the Oboloama civil war and the entire inhabitants of Olodiama were taken off by a smallpox epidemic. The two towns disappeared — all their inhabitants having died or emigrated.

Onyoama [4] must have been situated some distance from Oboloama and Olodiama, or its king must have been very clever, because it remained unaffected by their wars and plagues. Onyoama prospered, trading with the people of Kula to the east. People passed freely and safely between Onyoama and Kula. Then a prince of Kula fell in love with a princess of Onyoama. He wished to marry her and pressed to be introduced to the king of Onyoama. The princess considered it premature and enjoined patience. When the prince arrived on one of his trading trips, the princess was not at home. He was so anxious to meet his future father-in-law that he went to introduce himself. This was considered a breach of custom and etiquette. The King flew into a rage and, drawing his sword, slew the prince on the spot. When the princess returned and saw her lover's luggage without the man, she became apprehensive. Her attendants would not tell her what had happened. She hastened to the palace, only to see her lover's bleeding remains. She immediately set off for Kula singing a plaintive air:

> Onyoama, b'uru b'ēlē indi nēnge, b'uru na
> indi na gbōri b'ēlē, o mu b'ērē ko b'ie,
> Kula ntaba, idei nona tei gbania o? [5]

She told the king of Kula in graphic terms of the killing of his son and the reason for her earlier reluctance to introduce him to her father — she was awe-struck at the extreme comeliness of the prince and afraid for him because of her father's extreme bloodthirstiness. The king needed little urging to get his warriors ready for an attack on Onyoama. The war party gave the princess time only to withdraw her property from Onyoama before attacking. It was a complete victory for Kula, and Onyoama was razed to the ground.[6]

According to Tepowa, the survivors "repaired to the North-East of the country and established towns known as Segu, Sangana and Ekuleama." The head man of Ekuleama, Ekule, brought his people back to their original settlement and settled at Opupogu. The next group of settlers was a "race called Iselema [originally Benins]; they were fugitives from Benin who had fled the country on account of some offence."

The story of fugitive offenders from Benin (Oba-ama) is commonly told in Nembe. Mr. Tepowa's name for them — Iselema — invites comment, however. Iselema is actually the Nembe name for Warri and for the Itsekiri people. The text as it stands would be

equivalent to saying Warri people from Benin immigrated to Nembe.
The Itsekiri are indeed said to be descended from a Benin prince,
Ginuwa, and Warri to have been "a principality of Benin." [7] The
fugitives may thus have been subjects of the oba (king) of Benin
from the principality of Warri.

Tepowa renders the story of the fugitives as follows. The oba of
Benin sent an army to raid a stubborn town. He gave strict instructions that they were on no account to take his son with them. The
son, however, left a day ahead of the expedition and waited on the
way. When all members of the expedition refused to heed his appeals, the prince threatened to assault them unless they agreed to
let him go with them. He was accordingly taken along and was the
first to fall in the engagement. The men were afraid of the oba's
wrath. They returned home by night, packed their property, and
fled. They are said to have brought with them to Nembe "the male
god which they took to the war, leaving the female god at Benin."

The new arrivals were permitted to settle at Amasarapolo, but
the king of Nembe later changed his mind. He asked them to remove
their god to Oromabiri.

A further stream of immigrants also from Benin were called
"Obiamas." They came in search of fishing grounds but became
pirates — and a pest to the Ijaw and Nembe peoples. The Ijaw and
Nembe combined to wage war against them. They sued for peace
and permission to settle among the Nembe people. This was refused and they went down river to the coast and settled at the mouths
of the St. Nicholas, Brass, and Nun Rivers, "forming towns of their
own, known as Twon, Okpomo [Big Fish town], Iwama [Small
Fish town], Beletiama, Akassa, Odiama, Ologbobiri, and Ebelema."

Even after their removal downriver, the Nembe continued to
harass these coastal communities until they formally submitted. According to Tepowa, "it was in the days of the famous King Kulo
that these people [Obiama] enjoyed perfect freedom in Brass, and
up to this day the memory of King Kulo is green in the minds of
the Twon people, being always mentioned with sentiments of sin-
cere respect and affection." [8]

REVEREND OCKIYA'S ACCOUNT [9]

The Reverend D. O. Ockiya's account differs from Tepowa's in
several significant particulars. He insists that "a town or more" ex-

isted in the Nembe area before the arrival of Obolo, Onyo, and Olodia. He goes further, adding three names to these as founders of early settlements, namely, Opubiga, Kalabiga, and Oro (the founders of Opubigamabiri, Kalabigamabiri, and Oroamabiri). The first two were already established when Obolo, Onyo, and Olodia arrived. Their inhabitants were pirates according to the dictates of their god. They are also thought to have come originally from the neighboring Ogbia country.

The derivation of the name Oroamabiri from a man, Oro, is a departure from the popular account. The usual explanation of this name is that the juju priests from Warri (Iselema) were asked to move to this quarter of the town. The quarter was accordingly called Oru-ama-biri, meaning, juju quarter. Mr. Ockiya derives the name of the town from the name of the first priest — Oro. A further tradition given by Mr. Ockiya about the town of Oroamabiri connects its priests with the descendants of the princess of Onyoama who helped Kula to destroy her cruel father's kingdom. She was apparently expecting a child by the prince of Kula before he was killed by the king of Onyoama. After Onyoama was sacked she stayed on in Kula and gave birth to a baby daughter. This daughter was in turn married to a Kula prince. For some unknown reason, members of this family are said to have been appointed priests of the Nembe national god at Oroamabiri. The names of three such priests are given as Fengabala, Ago, and Agu.

After the dispersion of Oboloama, two brothers, Opu-Ekule (Ekule Senior) and Kala Ekule (Ekule Junior), led a party of men to found a town, Ekuleama, in the Kalabari district. Kala Ekule returned to build Nembe at Opupogu.

Mr. Ockiya differed most radically from Tepowa in his account of the immigration of the fugitive offenders:

. . . the following is the correct version as narrated to the author by Chief Apo of Big Warri on the 13th of August 1939 during his visit there: — The leader of the deserters to Nembe was a very rich man who had buried so many earthen pots full of coral beads in the ground to the knowledge only of his sister who was married to the then King, the Olu. He strictly warned her not to reveal it to any one, but somehow, she revealed the spot to her husband who went and dug them out to enrich himself. Not long after this, a war broke out between the

Itshekiris and Ovurugbo (a Soko town). The Olu called his brother-in-law and made him the head or captain of the fleet. The prince also accompanied them. When they came to the battlefield, they fought desperately, vanquished their enemies and burnt the town. To their surprise, however, the prince entered the King's palace and sat on the poisoned stool of the King, and got fastened to it. They tried all their possible best to take him on board their canoe, but failed. At last they were obliged to leave him there and proceed home. As they dared not enter the town for fear of being killed in cold blood by the Olu, they decided upon desertion; and so, having come to the town in the dead of night, they took away all their belongings with the male god which they took to the war and went as far as to Nembe for protection.

Further, their head or captain was of the family of one of the children of the two chiefs or councillors of Benin whom Nuwa the Oba of Benin sent with Prince Ginuwa his son in the Iroko Box to rule the Itshekiri kingdom and whose title was "Ibiegbe."

Having seen him and discussed him as advised by the Olu, Chief Apo and the other chiefs showed the author the female god and also the quarter left vacant by the deserters (still left uninhabited) and added that even then, they were still expecting the return of the Nembes.

The Olu entrusted the author with a message to the Nembe chiefs informing them that despite the homecall of the Rev. A. O. Ockiya [the Amanyanabo Mingi IX] to whom he had sent an invitation to be present at his coronation to perform a ceremony usually performed by the descendants of Ibiegbe but then still unperformed. He was still expecting them for the purpose in order to complete his coronation ceremony. On the return of the author, this message was delivered to the Nembe chiefs at a mass meeting held in the court hall on the 11th of Septemebr 1939.[10]

This story makes Nembe's connection with the Itshekiri very close indeed. The connection with Benin is accordingly derived merely through the Benin origin of the Itsekiri. Further, these Iselema or Warri immigrants arrived very early in the history of Nembe — in the time of Kala Ekule — and were accordingly one of the founding races. Rev. D. O. Ockiya gives the name of the Itsekiri war captain and descendant of Ibiegbe as Alepe, and tells that it was Alepe who was "afterwards known by the name of Nembe." He also makes Alepe the father of Ogbolo, Amasara, Bele, and Agbo, who gave their names to the quarters of Nembe — Amasarapolo, Beleupogu, Agbotubupolo — and also the name Ogbolomabiri. Amasarapolo,

Beleupogu, and Agbotubupolo would thus be the oldest quarters in Ogbolomabiri, the others — Tombi, Ockiya-Ewoama, and Isoukiri — being later settlements.

CONCLUSIONS ON ORIGIN OF NEMBE

To sum up the traditions, the nucleus of the Nembe people were the three settlements of Oboloama, Olodiama, and Onyoama. The three men, Obolo, Onyo, and Olodia, may have met indigenous settlements — probably of Ogbia descent. These indigenous peoples were either absorbed or displaced. In time the three nuclear settlements disappeared, some of their inhabitants moving into the Kalabari country to the east and northeast. A group of these immigrants from Oboloama, Olodiama, and Onyoama decided to return. Their leader was Kala-Ekule and he settled his men at Opupogu. Soon a further group of immigrants arrived from the west — Benin or Warri — and were received by Kala-Ekule. He gave them a quarter of his settlement, Amasarapolo, to settle in, but later asked all of them, or at least their priests, to move across the creek to Oromabiri. The later group of Benin or Warri or Ijaw immigrants were not absorbed into the metropolis, but were made to move further down towards the coast — the maritime settlements.

A few points about these legends may be discussed at this point. (1) The location of the three settlements — Oboloama, Olodiama, and Onyoama — and at which of them Kala-Ekule's settlement at Opupogu was located. (2) The nature of the Iselema or Benin immigration and what part these people eventually played in the creation of the state and its leadership. (3) The origin of the names of the people, the metropolis, and its quarters, arising from the legends of origin.

At the Ukelonu Commission of Inquiry (1959) a Bassambiri theory claimed that Ogbolomabiri represents the site of Oboloama, and Bassambiri that of Olodiama. Mr. Ockiya's account would also suggest that Kala-Ekule and his brother had moved to Ekuleama from Oboloama, and that he "returned" to Opupogu. This would place Opupogu in Oboloama. Tepowa also records that Ekuleama, from which Ekule came "back to Opupogu," was "a town formed by the Oboloama people and named after their headman Ekule." [11] Ogbolomabiri may thus be safely identified with Oboloama. It is not so certain, however, where Olodiama and Onyoama were. Their direction relative to Oboloama may however be deduced from the direction in which the tortoise and the python floated between Oboloama and Olodiama, and the fact that Onyoama was favorably placed for trade with Kula. From Opupogu (that is, a part of Oboloama), the ebb tide goes south and southwest, and the flood tide north. And for the Oboloama tortoise to get to Olodiama by flood tide, and for the Olodiama python to reach Oboloama by ebb tide, Olodiama had to be situated north of Opupogu. This position is not compatible with the present site of Bassambiri directly opposite Opupogu. Olodiama is likely to have been at the present site of Oromabiri or opposite it at the public cemetery of Ogbolomabiri or beyond it. Onyoama may have been south of both settlements.

The immigrants from Benin were warriors and brought with them the male war god, Ogidiga. Their leaders had been close to the Benin or Warri court and influential enough for the prince to follow or to seek to follow them on an expedition. They do not appear to have taken over the government or even to have attempted to do so. Ekule was able to move them from one quarter to another at will, and the town continued to be Kala-Ekulema Nembe. Alepe or his descendant's accession to authority must have been achieved by peaceful infiltration of the government through the exhibition of superior knowledge and talent for leadership. It was probably fear of similar tactics that prompted the rejection of the Obiama submission and the offer to settle in Nembe territory.

Alepe may have succeeded in winning control of the government, but it is unlikely that everything was thenceforth named after him and his sons. Tepowa's account agrees with Rev. D. O. Ockiya's in the view that the name Nembe derived "from Alepe, corrupted to Nembe." [12] The two words are easily pronounced by any Nembe man today and recognized as distinct and even dissimilar. There is no reason to accept this use of Alepe's name — and tradition recounts no outstanding achievements he may have made. The indication is that the name Nembe was in use during Ekule's reign, which would explain Ekule's apparent neglect in naming his settlement. If the name was in use, the suggestion that it derived from a fishing method becomes plausible. [13]

The derivation of the names Ogbolomabiri and Beleupogu from Alepe's sons Ogbolo and Bele is also open to doubt. It has been shown above that Ogbolomabiri — or at least Opupogu, where Ekule landed

— was part of Oboloama. A simple explanation would be that Ogbo-lomabiri was originally Oboloama-biri, that is, Oboloama quarter. The name could have been used to differentiate the quarter situated at the original site of Oboloama from the quarter of the Bassa traders, that is, Bassambiri.

The case against Bele is a simple one. Beleupogu means the first landing beach (b'ēlēu = first; pogu = landing beach). (See Note on Transliteration for diactric marks.) To mean Bele's landing beach, the name would have been Belepogu. It is the first version that is used now; this may represent the only instance of "corruption"— from Belepogu to Beleupogu.

If this analysis is correct, Alepe and his followers brought the war god, Ogidiga, new ideas of government, and the names Amasarapolo, Bele(u)pogu, and Oromabiri.

The Seacoast or Maritime Communities

The theory that the Nembe coastal settlements were the result of a wave of immigration different from the original founders of Nembe applies with special plausibility to the towns of Beletiema, Egwema, and Liama. These towns are situated in comparatively inaccessible parts of islands washed by the Atlantic. That is, the people appear to have moved down until there was no further ground for them to retreat to. These islands have a peculiarity of their own. The main settlement is placed in the heart of the island, protected by an outpost on the river front. Thus Beletiema is protected by Beletiema-pogu, and Egwema by Egwema-pogu. As a result either of their isolation or of their origin, Beletiema, Egwema, and Liama also have striking peculiarities in their speech. These towns are close to Akassa and their dialect may be a cross between Nembe and Akassa.

The towns of Okpoma, Twon, and Odioma are, however, more accessible and are obviously of the same origin as Nembe. Whatever differences that may have existed in the distant past have disappeared with close contact and intermarriage. In the case of Okpoma, the founder, Okpo, is said to have been a brother of Ogbolo (or Obolo), the founder of Ogbolomabiri.[14] The tradition at Okpoma is that both bothers emigrated from an Ijaw village, Obiama. There is no doubt, however, that Okpoma has been very closely identified with Ogbo-lomabiri throughout their recorded and remembered history. Okpoma has taken part in all major wars fought by the kings of Nembe. There is in fact the tradition, at both Nembe and Okpoma, that when Nembe went out on a campaign, hostilities could not begin until Okpoma had discharged the first shot. This was because the god of Okpoma, Kalaorowei, was the warlike son or flag bearer of Ogidiga, the national war god of the people. Further, a king-elect needed, after the normal ceremonies at Nembe, to go down to Okpoma in a state canoe for a special ceremony of recognition and acclamation by the people of Okpoma. A new king of Okpoma had similarly to go to Nembe after coronation at home.

The settlement of Twon apparently took its name from the outlandish speech of a stranger found on the beach. He is said to have been a fisherman from an Atlantic island (possibly Fernando Po) who got lost and was found wandering on the beach at the town known as Twon. When asked who he was and where he had come from, the stranger uttered unintelligible words from which the word Twon was derived.[15]

The town is now made up of the following sections or quarters: Imbikiri, Consulate, Kemmertown or Oruwarikiri, Twon, and Gbobokiri or Spiff's town. Imbikiri (kernel deport or settlement) and the consulate represent the section of the Brass River on which the "legitimate" traders built their "factories" and anchored their hulks — oliki. There are still parts of these hulks lying half-buried in the sand and visible at ebb tide. The name Imbikiri indicates the activities associated with this part of the town — the trade in palm oil and kernel. The Consulate is of course the part of the European settlement taken up by the British vice-counsel after 1891. It now comprises the offices and quarters of all government establishments.

Oruwarikiri (Kemmertown) and Gbobokiri (Spiff's town) were founded by persons from Nembe, and members of these places still retain their attachment to Houses in Nembe. Oruwari is of course the name of a prominent Nembe chief and the founder of the House of that name. Oruwarikiri means Oruwari's settlement, and it may have been established by Oruwari for the purposes of trade with the white men.

Gbobokiri was the place to which chief Ada Spiff fled during the civil war between Christians and their opponents at Nembe during the reign of Constantine Ockiya, Mingi VII (1863–79). Ada was warned of his danger and left Nembe by night. It is known that the

British consul at Fernando Po (Hopkins) and the white traders at Twon settled religious wars in Nembe between 1871–78.[16] The immigration to Gbobokiri may therefore have taken place in these years. Gbobo was Chief Ada Spiff's head representative and the settlement came to be known as Gbobokiri.[17]

The quarter named Twon may well be the most ancient part of the town, the one which most rightfully should give its name to the whole. It was, for some time, an insignificant place; most of the earlier travelers of the nineteenth century did not even mention it. Bishop Crowther visited it, however, on July 7, 1857, and wrote:

The village is in the swamps, and the inside of the houses very damp . . . the right side of the village is separated by a swamp, which is not easily crossed, except by wading through or being carried over it.

Thomas J. Hutchinson, consul for the Bight of Biafra (1855), wrote in his book, *Ten Years' Wondering Among the Ethiopians*, "The village of Twa contains about a hundred huts. This, however, is but a petty village." Twon's years of prosperity thus came with the beginning of British legitimate trade in palm oil and palm kernels, and later with the establishment of British administration. The traders bought and sold on the adjoining beaches. Chiefs from Nembe were attracted by the idea and built settlements. Later, the British administration established its headquarters for the entire Nembe area and beyond at the consulate. Twon became known as Brass — a name previously reserved for the indigenous metropolis of Nembe (Brasstown).

Expansion and Relation with Immediate Neighbors

The Ogbia clan to the north and northeast has been closely related to Nembe in the past. Many early anthropological reports have, in fact, asserted that when the first Nembe immigrants arrived from Benin, Iselema, or Ijaw there were already Ogbia settlers in the area.[18] These indigenous Ogbia are said to have been settled at Oromabiri and to have moved away when the Iselema were sent there. Olei, the founder of Oloibiri, is supposed, by these accounts, to have moved from Oromabiri. But this conflicts with the tradition of a common origin between the two subgroups of the Ogbia clan — Olei and Otokoroma. By this tradition, Olei came to Oloibiri from Ologoama in the Otokoroma area.[19]

The towns of Opomatubu, Amakalakala, and Akipelai, now classified as Ogbia, have had an even closer historical link with Nembe.
A 1932 report [20] noted that their connection with Nembe was "close
and of long standing" and that the people were bilingual in Nembe and Ogbia. The British, in 1895, had placed all three towns under
the Nembe native court system on the basis of this connection.

It is not clear, however, how far back the links of these towns to
Nembe or Ogbia go. In fact, the origin of Opomatubu is traceable to
sources distinct from either Ogbia or Nembe. Opomatubu tradition
relates it rather to the Odual clan farther north—the founder,
Opome, being a son of Odual, founder of the Odual clan. Opome,
however, traveled through Ogbia territory and so created the links
with Ogbia. The relation to Nembe came through military protection and intermarriage.

Clear traditional relations are traced between Nembe and the
Akassa clan at the Nun estuary west of the Brass River estuary. Akassa was an offshoot of the Apoi clan farther west whose founder,
Kalasuo, is thought to have belonged to the Benin war party that
escaped to settle in Nembe.[21] In time one of Kalasuo's men, Kassa,
established his own settlement—Kassama. La, the founder of Akassa, broke away from Kassama as the result of a quarrel over the
sharing of the soup of hare killed in communal hunting. La had
gone to his farm while the meat was cooking and was not given a
share. During the ensuing fracas, La and his entire following had
to leave Kassama.

La named his settlement Opu Akassa, after Kassa, but it was also
called Oginibiri. La's successor and son, Emere, moved away and
founded Etanghigbene, so named after a tree—*etanghi*—that grew
there. From these original villages the people expanded into their
present settlements.

The big Akassa town of Kamatoro or Sangana, however, has its
own history. It was founded by Ere, who arrived from Igbematoru
in the Ijaw clan of Bomo. He settled in Osiamabiri. In time people
arrived from Opu Akassa and added new quarters to the town. It
has become a completely Akassa town and lost all formal relation
with the Bomo clan. The headman of Sangana or Kamatoro, however, is still elected from among the descendants of Ere in Osiamabiri.

The age of the Akassa settlements has been the subject of conflicting estimates. A recent estimate based on the small number of

rulers since La indicated that the settlement was not of great antiquity.[22] In 1863, however, Sir Richard Burton thought Akassa was
an old town. He saw houses occupied by Portuguese traders in earlier
times, and also Portuguese graves dated 1635. The Portuguese connection was attested by other nineteenth-century explorers as a proof
of the town's age — although they mistook Portuguese influence for
Spanish. In 1832 Oldfield saw certain "Spanish" sheep the people kept
as fetish. In 1841 Allen and Thomson observed that the people of
Akassa "all, more or less spoke Spanish."

These nineteenth-century explorers also observed a close connection between Akassa and Nembe. There were many Nembe pilots
at Akass who dealt with the ships, and the visitors came to regard
Akassa as either a Nembe town or as one owing allegiance to the
rulers of Nembe. Dr. Baikie, however, in 1854, was told by a Nembe
man that Akassa was "an Oru village," that is, an Ijaw village.

To the east of Nembe are the peoples of Saka, Idema, Kugbo, and
others; these communities serve as buffers between Nembe and
Kalabari (New Calabar). The communities claimed the protection
of one of the rival states when threatened with attack from the other.
If the attackers were so near, however, that speedy help could not
be expected, they succumbed to the powerful neighbor. It was in
this manner that Okoroba, Idema, and Agrisaba came to be affiliated
to Bassambiri.

TRADITIONS OF COMMON DESCENT AMONG NIGER DELTA PEOPLES

Just as the various subgroups of Ijaw have a common language,[23]
so do they also have traditions of common descent. An analysis of
Nembe traditions shows that the Nembe have been intimately connected in turn with the Western Ijaw, Kalabari, Bonny, and Okrika;
and that all these groups are also interrelated.

Nembe relation with the Western Ijaw is evident from the fact
that both groups claim descent from Benin. The traditions of all
the peoples west of Nembe, indeed, indicate that they have all drifted
eastwards to their present locations from the general direction of
Benin.

With the Kalabari immediately to the east, Nembe tradition indicates not direct community of descent but rather a mixing. It would
appear that the eastward flow of peoples continued when the dispersed groups from Oboloama, Onyoama, and Olodiama settled at

Ekuleama in the Kalabari area. A certain Kala-Ekule returned to the Nembe area, but he apparently left some of the original migrants behind.

Nembe and Bonny traditions show possibilities of an eastward spill from Nembe being responsible for or at least contributing to the founding of Bonny. But supernatural sanctions rather than traditions of common descent are often cited to explain the fact that no wars are ever known to have been fought between the two states of Brass and Bonny. The Nembe god Ogidiga and the Bonny god Ekiba are said to be related in spiritland and cannot, therefore, make war against each other.[24]

Traditions of common descent are particularly strong between Nembe and Okrika. Tradition at both places suggests that Ogulaya, the founder of Ogulama (Ogoloma), came from one of the early Nembe settlements.[25] The city of Okrika itself was assigned by Ogulaya to one of his men, Oputibeye. Oputibeye's settlement was to serve as a buffer against Mbolli attacks. When Oputibeye protested against this use of his settlement, Ogulaya assured him of continued support from Ogulama, saying *wa kirike* — "we are not different." And *kirike* was eventually corrupted to Okrika.

The traditions of common descent of Okrika and Nembe are supported by the evidence of their religion. The python which is worshipped as a symbol of Ogidiga at Nembe also appears in the worship of Ogoloma. Some parts of Okrika no longer venerate the python, but these people are said to be immigrants from the hinterland, after Oputibeye.[26]

INTERRELATIONS

It is reasonable to conclude from the striking similarity in language, customs, and tradition that at some remote date a nuclear Ijaw people were thinly spread all over the Delta from the River Ramos to the River Opobo. The present differences in dialect, culture, and tradition may then represent the result of later infiltration of new elements and of the geographical isolation of the various groups. Leonard, who studied Delta traditions of origin, was also impressed with the interrelations between the groups, but he could not suggest a firm common bond. He concluded

That the Ibani, i.e., the Bonny and Opobo people, although they trace their origin to an Ibo and can speak that tongue, also claim connection

with Brass. That the New Calabar [Kalabari] natives appear to have
been a combination of Efik from Creek town and of Ijo on the coast,
who divided into three sections— one remaining as the New Calabar,
the other two separating in the direction of Brass and Bonny. That
nothing is known about the Ijo, except the question of their Bini [Benin]
descent, which, however, rests on the slenderest of evidence.[27]

The evidence of tradition would suggest that the nuclear group
spread across the Delta from west to east, and that the later infiltrat-
ing immigrants came mainly from the Ibo and Efik hinterland to
the north and east.

The Nature of Benin Influence in the Delta

It has been suggested that the claim to Benin origin by many
Delta peoples may be no more than a proof of the widespread influence and the prestige of the Oba of Benin.[28] In Nembe all folk tales
and fables begin with the preface that the events related happened
once upon a time in "Obaama" (Oba's town, i.e., Benin). Certain
nursery chants sung by mothers to lull their children to sleep contain
words which no longer mean anything in Nembe but which include
the name Ado—the word for the ancient empire of Benin.[29] There
is also the proverb: *Ado bebe naghabo ikioikio eke Ado bebe na*—
"a man who does not understand the Bini [Benin] language may
yet know what is spoken by sheer common sense." These things
which have become a part of language and tradition would suggest
that the claims to Benin origin need not always be unfounded.

At the other extreme, there is the view, originating from early
Portuguese maps, that the boundaries of the Benin Empire extended
eastward to Bonny.[30] The evidence of oral tradition is that the authority of the Oba did not penetrate the Delta. The Delta rather
served as a refuge for people who sought to escape the power of
Benin. Even as a refuge, Nembe or the Brass area seems to have been
the limit of direct penetration by these fugitives from the Benin
Empire.

The political authority of Benin may, indeed, have reached no
farther into the Delta than Warri at any time. But even this limited
extension into the Delta is denied by one of William Bosman's cap-
tains at the beginning of the eighteenth century. Writing of the
River Formosa or Benin in 1702, Nyendael says:

The inhabitants of this river, and the neighbouring country, have several Princes; and, indeed, each small nation is governed by his own King, though all of them are vassals to the King of Benin, except those of Awerri [Warri], where the Portuguese live, and the pirates of Usa [Ijaw], both of whom would never submit to his yoke.[31]

4

EARLY HISTORY

King List and Chronology

The most convenient indication of time in oral history is the length of reigns of kings. Events are dated by the name of the king in whose reign they occurred. A comparison of various king lists (see Appendix I) shows that the following represents the kings of Nembe from the time after the dispersal of Oboloama, Olodiama, and Onyoama and the return of Kala-Ekule from Ekuleama.

Early Kings

Ekule (*circa* 1450–1500)	Ogio
Ogbodo	Peresuo
Nembe	Obia
Owagi	Basuo (*circa* 1700)

Kings of *Ogbolomabiri*	Kings of *Bassambiri*
Mingi I	Ogbodo
Ikata — [Mingi] II	Gbolowei
Gboro III	Dede
Kulo (King Forday) IV	Tamuno
(1800–32)	Kariyai
Amain (King Boy) V	Mein (King Jacket)
(1830–46)	Duguruyai
Kien VI (1846–63)	Arisimo (King Peter d. 1870)

Ockiya VII (1863–79)

Koko VIII (1889–98)

Anthony Ockiya IX
  (1926–36)

Francis O. Joseph Alagoa X
  (1954–   )

Ebifa (1870–94)

Albert Oguara (1924–27)

Ben I. Warri (1928–   )

Kala-Ekule's reign has been estimated to have fallen in the period 1450–1500. This estimate was made from the average length of reigns from the part of the king list for which the dates are firm, that is, between Kulo, Mingi IV and Mingi X. Dr. Dike's conclusions on the peopling of the Niger Delta would suggest that the dates 1450–1500 given for Ekule are too recent. Dr. Dike has said that "The immigrations from Benin were . . . prefifteenth century, and took place possibly centuries before the advent of the Portuguese."[1] If, as is known, the Portuguese dealt with fully established states when they arrived at Delta ports like New Calabar (Kalabari) in the second half of the fifteenth century, it is reasonable to suppose that the bulk of the immigrations took place either before or very early in the fifteenth century.

If Ekule's establishment of the monarchy is thus placed early in the fifteenth century, the arrival of Obolo, Onyo, and Olodia must be estimated for at least a century earlier. No shorter span may be allowed for the history of Oboloama, Onyoama, and Olodiama, because as many as nine kings are listed for Oboloama alone.[2]

LIVES OF THE EARLY KINGS

Little is known of the lives of the kings between Ekule and Basuo beyond their names. Ekule, for example, is known simply as "the first king of Nembe after the return of the Ekuleama to Nembe."[3] Even less is known about his son Ogbodo, about Ogbodo's son Nembe, or about Nembe's successor, Owagi.[4]

The entire genealogy of the kings, however, is remembered from the fifth king, Ogio. He has also given his name to the public square — *ogio polotiri* — where funeral rites are performed for persons without taint of witchcraft.[5]

Ogio's son and successor, Peresuo, is obscure as a personality, and two of his sons, Obia and Basuo, ruled after him. The first recorded war was fought by King Basuo against Koloama, a Bassa town. This king also showed himself no respector of persons by drowning his cousin Chief Opo for his "atrocious deeds." [6]

THE CIVIL WAR (ca. 1700)

According to Tepowa, no king could be appointed after the death of Basuo because the children of the two brothers, who were named Ogbodo and Mingi, both claimed the crown. Then an unexpected quarrel between the sons of Mingi and Ogbodo at a game of *egian* led to violence between the rival parties and the death of a son of Ogbodo. He was the first buried on Iwofe-Sara ("the hill of those who die young by accident or violence"). The people, however, favored Ogbodo for the throne and Mingi retired to Ondewari. Mingi became great friends with the king of Ondewari and persuaded him to join in a war of blockade and piracy against Ogbodo. A great famine resulted in Nembe, and Ogbodo himself crossed to Oromabiri and advised the people to offer the throne to Mingi.

Mingi rejected the first offer and moved to Tereke where he began to train to be a blacksmith. He became rich and loved by the people of the area, but was hated by the king and people of Ologoama. He was invited to Ologoama and plans made to murder him. This was revealed to Mingi by one of the king's wives — a mother-in-law of Mingi — and he left Ologoama in a hurry. Nobody would stop him because "Mingi was very stout, and tall — indeed, gigantic; he could lift and throw a man with one hand, he was repulsive in appearance and stammered in speech; he was also very passionate and extremely cruel."

The Ologoama people continued to conspire; and, on being warned of a second attempt on his life, Mingi packed up and went to Okpoma. The people of Nembe sent again to press him to become king, and he finally consented and was proclaimed king. Ogbodo had meanwhile obtained permission from the elders to establish a homestead at Bassambiri — the village on the side of Bassa-town.

In Tepowa's account, Mingi, though proclaimed king, was not crowned formally. He accordingly forbade the making of chiefs in his reign. He also drove the people of Odioma to the protection of Ogbodo and his followers in Bassambiri. At the instigation of Chief Orukare of Okpoma, Mingi seized all Odioma people who came to a festival at Nembe and sold them into slavery. Tepowa concludes about Mingi: "The only redeeming feature in the reign of this cruel king was the establishment of agriculture in Nembe for it was reported that he ordered Tubo Piri to be cleared and set aside exclusively for that purpose; after this was done he placed it in charge of Imeku." [7]

THE DIVIDED KINGDOM

Ogbodo, the first king of Bassambiri, would appear to have been a peace-loving man, and while his cousin is sometimes referred to as Mingi the Great, Ogbodo is called the peacemaker. It is not surprising, therefore, that people who were dissatisfied with Mingi should come over to Ogbodo — as the Odioma did. Ogbodo would also appear to have established a system of peaceful co-existence with his cousin. Still, it may be doubted if Ogbodo was a completely successful leader. His inability to retain the combined throne after his rival had been driven out remains unexplained. He appears to have been so unsuccessful that the people went to the extent of sending repeated offers of the crown to Mingi, who could afford to feign reluctance to accept. Even in Bassambiri he is known only for setting up the settlement; the real hero is a later ruler, Mein, who was a contemporary of King Forday Kulo of Ogboloamabiri.

The successors of Ogbodo and Mingi engaged in further hostilities. King Ikata, son of Mingi, attempted to close all food markets to Bassambiri traders. Gbolowei, son and successor of Ogbodo, made farms on the back of Bassambiri and resisted the blockade. There was apparently a stalemate and the blockade was called off.

In other ways King Ikata is represented as being more nearly the ideal monarch. Although he stuttered like his father, he was without his father's short temper. Unlike his father and his successors, he never applied the full legal penalty of drowning for his adulterous wives, or for those suspected of adultery. Ikata is remembered for his leadership in war, and is even reported to have introduced the idea of the war canoe either at this time or before the outbreak of the Bila war. Though gallant in war, he was humane and refused to execute his war captives in sacrifice as was the custom. This is given as the reason King Ikata's memorial hall (okpu) backs the public square (opupolotiri) where the peri pele play is enacted.

THE BILA WAR (Ca. 1770–80)

Once upon a time King Ikata sent men to trade with the Europeans stationed at Bonny and Kalabari (New Calabar). On their way back King Amakiri of Kalabari gave the men an ivory bowl as a present to King Ikata. As the Nembe men were passing through the town of Bila, the inhabitants attacked them, killing some and seizing others to be sold into slavery. Two of the men, one of them a grandson of Mingi, were snatched away from the scene of disaster by a spirit disguised as a man. They were mysteriously left at the town of Ke (reputed to be the oldest town in the Delta.) [8] The two men told their sad tale and the king and people of Ke took pity on them.

The king of Ke took good care of them while they were in Ke and sent messengers to take them safely home with presents for King Ikata. Ikata was so grateful that he sent presents of great value by the messengers back to their king.

King Ikata took no immediate action to redress the wrong done him by the people of Bila. Two years passed and he had still done nothing — manifesting an apparent reluctance to go to war that has been attributed to the fact that King Jike of Bila was Ikata's cousin. This inactivity incensed his sister Ingo. She stormed into the king's palace one day and struck him on the cheek, breaking the pipe he was smoking. She railed at him, urging him to be a man, and saying that had she been a man she would not be so supine. King Ikata was roused to action.

In one of the war canoes belonging to Chief Imeku was a famed medicine man, Elelekwe, who had lived a long time among the Bila and knew all about their god. He foretold the destruction of Bila.

The Nembe fleet had to lie in ambush for three days without being able to draw the enemy out. Finally they threw out all the refuse in the canoes, and when the Bila saw the flotsam on the river they concluded that the Nembe men of war had struck camp. They came into the open, and the battle commenced.

The slaughter on the Bila side is said to have been heavy — so heavy that the hands of the slain were later hung from one end of Nembe to the other. The losses to King Ikata's fleet was only one man killed in Chief Ogbari's canoe.

King Ikata, however, was not interested in the general slaughter. He sought to meet his cousin, King Jike, in single combat. He pursued him so closely that King Jike had to throw out a young man as offering to the gods of the river, calling out —"I am innocent, for I did reprimand my people, but they would not listen to me." King Ikata then fired a shot after him which blinded Jike in one eye, but he failed to catch him. King Ikata was so mortified by his failure to kill or capture Jike that his head was bowed all the way from the scene of action back to Nembe. This did not, however, prevent him from taking the grand praise title: *Jike bei na munate, Jike bei toru mi ten kpawomo, Osuokoromo Bila ba* — "related to Jike, blinded him by a gun shot, caused rain to slay the Bila." (The action was fought under a downpour.)

Early Developments

The evidence of oral tradition regarding the early kings throws light on some important subjects. It may be noted that there was no approach to large-scale farming in Nembe until the reign of Mingi in Ogbolomabiri and Gbolowei in Bassambiri. This lack of self-sufficiency underlines the importance of trade with the Bassa Ijaw and with Kalabari. The few external wars that were fought in the eighteenth century were obviously trade wars — the Koloama and Bila being communities on trade routes.

It may be noted, too, that the monarchy under Ikata was self-confident and that Ikata exchanged presents with other rulers of the Delta. King Amakiri of Kalabari was at about this time (1770–91) engaged in rivalry with King Pepple of Bonny (1760–92) for the control of the trade with the white man. King Amakiri's presents may have been intended to make an ally against the rising power of Bonny.[9] Nembe was probably then a desirable ally and not yet a rival since internal struggle between Ogboloamabiri and Bassambiri was not conducive to a spectacular role in the external politics of the Delta.

5

TRADE AND POLITICS ON
THE BRASS RIVER

It is known that the Portuguese arrived on the Nigerian coast before 1485. By that date they had identified "five slave rivers"[1]—the Mahin (Rio Primeiro or First River), Benin (Rio Formosa), Escravos, Forcados, and Ramos.

Talbot lists a further eight rivers in the eastern Delta said to have been known to the Portuguese traders between 1472–1600.[2] Talbot's list does not contain the names of the three estuaries of the Brass area, the Nun, Brass, and St. Nicholas. Three early Dutch maps (1513, 1619, 1699) reproduced by Talbot[3] also present a confused picture of that part of the coast. The 1513 map names no rivers in this area, while the 1619 map inserts a name, R. S. Lemto, between Cape Formosa and the River Bartholomew. The 1699 map makes up for the earlier omission by inserting the names of four rivers: (1) Rio Non (Benito); (2) Rio Oddy (or Fonsoady, or Mofonsa); (3) Rio Tilana (S. Juan), which is not given a very clear estuary but placed very close to the preceding one; (1) Rio Sto. Nicholas (Lempta, Juan Dias).

Barbot, who reproduced the 1699 map in his book, also named four rivers in this area in describing the coast between Cape Formosa and the New Calabar River. They are, first, the Nun; second, the Brass; fourth, the St. Nicholas. The third is non-existent:

The first of the seven rivers that show themselves in this tract of land, is Rio Non, four leagues east of Cape Fermosa.

The second river, farther east, is Rio Oddy, or Malfonsa, or Fonsoady, or S. Bento, remarkable, being south of it, in seven fathom water, from two tall capes or heads it has on both sides of its mouth; the land within the heads being flat and low: there are also two thickets of trees, high and lofty, on the east side of the river, not far from each other; the coast low and level.

The third is that of Filana or Juan Dias.

The fourth is that of S. Nicholas or Lempta.[4]

It is obvious from the wealth of names given to single estuaries, that much confusion prevailed in the naming of rivers. In a list of the "mouths of the Kwora," Baikie set down the various names by which the three estuaries of the Brass coast were known. The River Nun was Rio Non and the First Brass River. The Brass River itself was St. John, Second Brass River, Rio Bento, Malfonsa, Oddy, Fonsaody. The St. Nicholas was Rio di San Nicholas, Rio di Filana or Tilana, Rio di Juan Diaz, Sempta or Lempta.

The absence of the three Brass estuaries in the earlier lists does not prove that these rivers were unknown to the Portuguese. Barbot's detailed description of the Brass River shows that it was well known. It only represents the degree of importance attached to these areas for trade. The Kalabiri or New Calabar area was the center of trade in the Delta at this early period, and the ships passed straight from the Benin area to New Calabar. Barbot, continuing the above description, confirms this: "At all the above mentioned rivers small ships may anchor, and try their fortune, for getting some slaves, and elephant's teeth; but the most probable is Rio Sombreiro."

SLAVE TRADE

The slave trade had an early start in the Brass River as on other neighboring rivers. It does not, however, appear to have ever become as important as centers like New Calabar and later Bonny. The boom years for the slave trade on the Brass River only came in the second quarter of the nineteenth century when British blockade of the other rivers became effective.

Nembe's remoteness from the sea then became an advantage and it developed as the center of the Portuguese and Latin American slave trade.[5] When Richard and John Lander arrived at Nembe in 1830, the first white person they saw was a Spanish slave dealer. One Don Pablo Frexas was actually resident there and organized a smuggling trade despite the activities of the British squadron. Don Pablo died at Bonny in 1842, but the Brass River continued to be the virtual preserve of Portuguese and Spanish slave traders for at least the rest of the decade.[6]

Colonel (later General Sir) Edward Nicolls, governor of Fernando Po (1829–34), is said to have signed a "Treaty Offensive and Defensive" with King Boy Amain in 1834. In the absence of a prosperous trade in other commodities, King Boy did nothing to hinder the slave trade on the Brass River. In any case, the British government itself as good as repudiated this and other treaties made by Nicolls when it recalled him.

The Portuguese left a great impression on the coastal trade system. They gave names to the various rivers and their trade terms survived. They arrived on the coast in their ships and lived on them until a full load was collected. If a chief was friendly or wished to extend the trade in his area, yards and stores were provided on shore for the slaves. These were the barrikos or barracoons.

The chiefs at the coast obtained their slaves from the hinterland. These slaves served two purposes: as domestic servants, and as wives to increase the size and strength of the chief's Houses, and as a source of revenue on sale to the white traders. De Cardi,[7] who claims to have interviewed slaves and made a special study of the system as it operated in the Brass area, lists several ways in which slaves were obtained. A slave may have changed hands as many as four times before he got to the coast. He might originally be captured in a raid between villages. Women and children might be taken while they were going to a spring or wandering in a nearby bush. Or the slave catcher might approach with a gaudy and enticing present. Still others were sold by their parents, brothers, and uncles for debt, or saved by priests from sacrifice.

INTERNAL TRADE, MARKETS

Trade with the white man did not constitute the whole economic life of the Nembe people. It is clear that there were wide trading activities around the Niger Delta and with peoples in the direct hinterland before the arrival of the white man. The trade with the white man was, in fact, fed from markets and contacts long established to satisfy internal needs.

The geographical circumstances of the Niger Delta ensured that the Brass people would resort to trade to obtain the foodstuffs it was impossible to grow in their own surroundings. Richard Lander remarked in 1830: "The principal employment of the people consists in making salt, fishing, boiling oil, and trading to the Ebo country." These were the activities providence appears to have marked out for Delta peoples. Most Delta villages had and have small plantations of plantains, coconuts, cassava, and bananas, but these were insufficient to feed the whole population. It was necessary to barter the products of local industry with the agricultural products of the hinterland.

Salt-making and fishing have been the most ancient activities peculiar to the Ijaw communities in the Delta. Richard Lander saw in Nembe special huts for the manufacture of salt, which was exchanged for food in the up-country markets. Tradition indicates that entire villages had been set aside for the salt industry or had specialized in it. One such center was the village of Fantuo — a name which itself may have been a corruption of futuo (fu: salt; tuo: boil). The most ancient method appears to have been that of extracting the salt concentrated in the aerial roots of the mangrove tree. These branchlike roots were collected and burned to ashes. The ashes were then stirred in clear water and, by a complicated process of filtration and evaporation, a special brand of salt was obtained. Little knowledge of the process now remains. Later, sea water was found to be a cheaper source of salt.

Fishing has remained a major occupation supporting trade. Laird and Oldfield in 1832 considered the people "expert at spearing fish," reporting that "their harpoons are about eight feet long, are loaded at the end and are thrown with considerable force and accuracy." [8]

A third important industry was the making of dugout canoes. The people of Egwema and Odioma are noted for their proficiency, and their canoes are sold widely in the Delta.

MARKETS

The Delta confluence town of Aboh, the "Eboe country" of the Landers, was the focal point of big trading. Occasionally, canoes might pass on to Onitsha, and possibly to Idah and Lokoja.[9] The normal practice, however, was for Delta traders to collect products from the north and the Ibo hinterland at Aboh.

On the east, the Nembe trading area touched the Kalabari markets in the Oguta Lake district. In the western Delta, what were known as "the Assay markets" on the Warri River were most important for domestic supplies.[10] A cassava product of this area, farina (*ifenia* in Nembe), has become the staple breakfast diet of the Nembe people. Two towns in the Warri area — Okpari and Ivorogbo — are now the main supply centers, although oral history indicates that the Bassa Ijaw to the west had been the original suppliers. At a time when the capital of Nembe was still unified, the Bassa traders used to display their farina in the quarter now named Bassambiri (meaning Bassa quarter).

The activities of the Bassa underline the fact that her immediate neighbors to the west and north — the Ijaw and Ogbia — have been Nembe's best friends. These peoples grow plantains, cocoyam, and sugar cane and collect palm produce. In the 1890's one of the bitterest complaints against the Royal Niger Company, Chartered and Limited, was to be against the company's prevention of internal trade in foodstuffs with the Ijaw.

It is often declared that the coastal middlemen were completely opposed to European entry into the hinterland. The chiefs on the Brass River were not opposed to all contact between the white man and the producers. They made, instead, a clear definition of market spheres. King Ockiya's policy in 1876 was, first, that the Europeans go farther inland than Brass canoes could reach, and second, that they trade in "a different kind of produce." In terms of the Niger, the king said: "What we want is, that the markets we have made between the river and Onitsha should be left to ourselves."

"Legitimate" Trade

The British took the lead in the war against the slave trade and accordingly became the pioneers of the trade in palm oil. The "legitimate," "equitable," or "honorable" trade in commodities other than human beings gathered momentum in the Oil Rivers of the Nigerian coast in the 1830's, but it did not become important on the Brass River until the 1850's.

In 1830, the Landers were surprised that, while Brass was much closer to the Aboh markets "where the best palm oil was to be had," Bonny had become the coastal center of the trade. Their explanation was the dangerous bar of the river — out of five English vessels that had entered the river prior to this, three had struck the bar.

By 1856, however, the picture had changed: the Brass River had become one of the oil trading areas. For the period January 1, 1855, to January 1, 1856, a total of 2,280 tons of palm oil was exported from the river; [12] and in 1857 "as many as a hundred Brass River canoes" were observed at the port of Twon, "each carrying six puncheons of palm oil." [13] By 1864, the annual export figure for the Brass River was put at 2,000–2,800 tons, as against 4,500–5,000 for Old Calabar, and 16,000–17,000 for Bonny and New Calabar (Kalabari) together. [14] And by this time the Delta was yielding £800,000 out of the total African annual palm oil export of £1,500,000.

From about 1876, however, Brass River trade in palm oil had begun to feel the effect of European competition in the hinterland markets. After 1886 the position became desperate for the local middlemen as a result of the monopolistic activities of the Royal Niger Company at Akassa. Traders on the Brass River, however, did some purposeful smuggling against the regulations of the company and the following figures are given for the imports and exports on the Brass River in 1891–93. [15]

Year	Imports	Exports
	(£)	(£)
1891–92	40,500	65,500
1892–93	52,000	104,000

The Akassa Raid came in 1895 after a particularly lean year (1894) when the Royal Niger Company succeeded in tightening its control system and also bought up what British competition there still was at Brass. Political tension was reduced after the Kirk Commission and after the company's charter was taken away in 1900, but the Brass River gradually lost its importance as a trading area. Table 2 and Table 3 show the final decline of commercial activity in the ports of Brass and Akassa from 1895 to 1901. (The particular measures adopted by the Royal Niger Company to keep Brass river merchants from the Niger markets, and the rates of duties it imposed, are given in Chapter 7 as part of the story of the Akassa War. [16])

For the port of Twon, Brass, the decline in trade was due, in part, to the presence of the Royal Niger Company at Akassa only a few miles away. The company's monopoly made it unprofitable for the supercargoes to operate at Brass and trade began to flow to the eastern Delta — to the Kalabari port of Abonnema on the River Sombreiro, and to Bonny. The construction of modern port facilities at Port Harcourt in 1914 put a seal on this eastward flow of trade from the Brass River.

Akassa did not fare much better after the Niger Company's charter was abrogated in 1899. It was soon found that the River Forcados, and not the Nun on which Akassa stands, was the main stream to the Niger. The company accordingly began a gradual withdrawal

TABLE 2

Quantity and Value of Exports from Brass and Akassa for Six Years, Ended March 31, 1901

| | Ivory | | Palm Kernels | | Palm Oil | | Rubber | | Other Articles | Total |
Year	Quantity (lbs.)	Value (£)	Quantity (lbs.)	Value (£)	Quantity (lbs.)	Value (£)	Quantity (lbs.)	Value (£)	Value (£)	Values (£)
1895–96	–	–	1,320	9,130	203,233	8,836	–	–	742	18,708
1896–97	–	–	1,297	9,548	169,270	7,457	–	–	950	17,955
1897–98	–	–	1,323	11,222	211,548	9,908	–	–	270	21,400
Average	–	–	1,313	9,966	194,683	8,733	–	–	654	19,353
1898–99	–	–	1,363	10,191	250,363	11,623	–	–	138	21,952
1899–1900	–	–	1,592	12,222	176,636	9,463	–	–	103	21,788
1900–01	43	11	4,617	37,846	537,544	41,052	8,046	423	1,918	81,250
Average	14	4	2,524	20,086	431,544	20,713	2,682	141	720	41,664

Average value of imports for 1895–98 was £15,081.

Average value for imports for 1898–1901 was £39,943.

Source: NA/E, CSE. 1/1/1. Appendixes to Report by H. L. Searle, Collector of Customs, to Secretary, Southern Provinces, 1901.

to Forcados. By 1906 the dock had been moved and, in 1933, the customs house and post office.

The decline of trade on the Rivers Nun and Brass was, of course, aided by a natural cause — the danger of the bar of which the supercargoes had complained since the 1830's. The bar of these rivers has not become better; it would appear, rather, to be silting up. It was for this reason that the Nigerian government refused to include the dredging of the Nun in its 1946–56 Ten-Year Development Plan. It was argued that it would require constant dredging to keep an open navigable stream on the Nun and Brass Rivers.

TABLE 3

Return Showing the Number and Tonnage of Vessels Entered and Cleared at Each Port of Southern Nigeria from April 1, 1900, to March 31, 1901, and the Corresponding Period of 1899–1900

Ports	1900–1901 Entered		1900–1901 Cleared		1899–1900 Entered		1899–1900 Cleared	
	No.	Registered tonnage	No.	Registered tonnage	No.	Registered tonnage	No.	Registered tonnage
Old Calabar	103	187,531	102	185,271	88	144,278	85	140,960
Opobo	43	72,677	43	70,577	46	79,835	46	79,947
Bonny	134	239,947	131	235,392	83	145,489	82	143,072
New Calabar[a]	29	49,020	28	47,190	44	69,558	44	69,558
Brass	47	72,504	48	76,017	41	70,799	41	70,799
Akassa	41	61,652	39	61,454	6	7,555	6	7,555
Warri [b]								
Benin and Sapele	245	247,622	247	246,148	147	197,879	148	199,801
Forcados								
Total for all ports	642	930,953	638	922,049	455	715,393	452	711,692

[a] Closed as Port of Entry October 1900; all vessels entering and clearing at Bonny.

[b] All vessels cleared at Forcados.

Source: NA/E, CSE 1/1/1. Appendixes to Report by H. L. Searle, Collector of Customs, to Secretary, Southern Provinces, 1901.

COURTS OF EQUITY: COMMERCIAL LAW

Courts of equity were associations organized by the super-cargoes on the Oil Rivers to settle commercial disputes. A British Consul had been appointed at Fernando Po in 1849 (John Beecroft), but he proved unable to exercise authority sufficient to determine quickly in cases between the supercargoes and the Delta middlemen, or between the supercargoes on the coast. The supercargoes accordingly took the initiative in forming what Dr. Baikie called "a commercial or mercantile association" at Bonny in 1854. The Bonny court of equity was well run even at this early date: "The members being the Chief white and black traders in the place, and the chair occupied by the white supercargoes in monthly rotation. All disputes were brought before this Court . . . and with the consent of the King, fines are levied on defaulters. If anyone refuses to submit to the decision of the Court, or ignores its jurisdiction, he is tabooed, and no one trades with him. The natives stand in much awe of it, and readily pay their debts when threatened with it." [17]

The court of equity, Brass River, was established before 1870. In that year the revival of a case previously settled by the Brass court of equity at the colonial court at Cape Coast raised the general question of the competence of all courts of equity.[18] Such cases and the need to strengthen the hands of consuls led to the issue of the Order-in-Council of February 21, 1872. The Order named the rivers then served by courts of equity as Old Calabar, Bonny, Cameroons, New Calabar, Brass, Opobo, Nun, and Benin. The courts were "to be composed of British agents and traders." Any British trader refusing to enroll as a member was to forfeit the right to protection. It was lawful "for the Court of equity, but subject to the sanction of the consul, . . . to hear and determine any suit of a civil nature . . . between a British subject and a subject of the native chief or chiefs. . . ."

A record of the proceedings of the Brass court of equity for the years 1883–91 shows that it enjoyed less prestige among the chiefs than did the Bonny court. This was probably due in part to the fact that on the Brass River none of the chiefs was enrolled as a permanent member of the court of equity. The chiefs were invited to attend only when their assistance was needed or when they preferred complaints against one of the trading firms or their servants. The

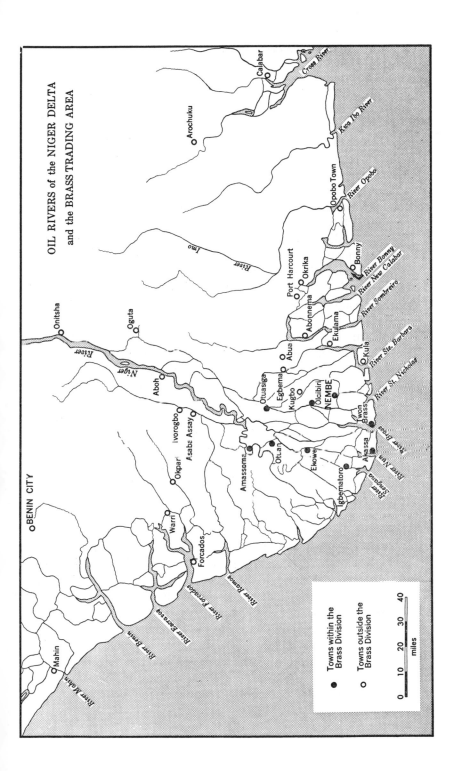

OIL RIVERS of the NIGER DELTA
and the BRASS TRADING AREA

Towns within the Brass Division
Towns outside the Brass Division

miles
0 10 20 30 40

chiefs accordingly treated the court as a foreign institution. One example will suffice to show the peremptory manner in which the chiefs considered it necessary to address the court.

At the court's meeting of August 19, 1885, it was reported that the chiefs had ordered three of the traders to sell their launches, pay a fine of 100 puncheons, and to sign a bond not to go "beyond Fishtown Point on the one side and Akassa Creek on the other." The traders so ordered were also admonished to report any others who attempted to go upriver without permission. The court could do nothing to help their colleagues but to write an urgent appeal to the nearest British naval commander. It took Commander Craigie himself two months to settle the quarrel, and then he had to take "a political prisoner." In the end the chiefs made a security deposit of "forty puncheons for good behaviour," and the traders signed a further bond to observe the embargo on trade in "the native markets."

The action of the chiefs was an attempt to enforce the policy outlined by King Ockiya in 1876: that the European traders must be kept out of markets in the interior unless they were willing to go beyond Onitsha, and willing also to buy produce other than those the Nembe traders bought.

If the Brass court of equity did not enjoy the confidence and respect of the local chiefs, neither did it enjoy the cooperation of all the agents or supercargoes on all occasions. During a crucial meeting of the court to work out ways of combating the chiefs' embargo on trade, one of the agents, Mr. Tasker, was absent, "and giving no reason for same." It is clear that the chiefs found it possible, on occasion, to use the rivalries of the various firms against the authority of the court.

There were instances, however, when the interests of the chiefs and the white traders on the Brass River coincided, and both parties then worked through the agency of the court of equity. Such an instance was the challenge presented to Brass River commerce by the establishment of the National African Company, Ltd. (Royal Niger Company after 1886) on the neighbouring Nun estuary at Akassa. That company not only posed a problem of straight competition, but also the threat of exclusion of all Brass River interests from markets on the River Niger. In November and December of 1885, the court of equity wrote letters of protest to the mercantile interests of the Liverpool African Association. It was shown that the National African Company had begun to carry treaties purporting to award it "sole right of Trading, Mining, Farming, Building, and even sole administrative powers . . ." on the Niger. To disprove these claims, the court submitted a protest signed by "Obe Najong, King of all Onitsha," together with twenty-seven chiefs and Queen Omu.

The court's reaction, first, to the local threat of the chiefs, and second, to the threat of the National African Company, reveals the anomalous nature of the British authority that was the ultimate sanction for the court's decisions. To deal with the purely local threat of the chiefs, the court appealed to the consul or to officers of the British squadron on the coast. Before 1885 the consul was supposed to be dealing with the Oil River states as the representative of one power to another sovereign nation. The "gunboat" activities of the naval officers was then justified by such phrases as "the suppression of the slave trade," "service to legitimate commerce," "justice," and "humanity." After the British government proclaimed the Oil Rivers Protectorate in June 1885, the use of British power in the service of British traders was justified, to the local chiefs, on the grounds of the protectorate declaration. Thus Commander Craigie began his interview with the chiefs, over their embargo on trade in the interior markets, by reading the declaration.

While the British used the unilateral protectorate declaration as a basis for the exercise of authority over the Delta states, they still thought it necessary to go through the motions of obtaining consent. In Brass, Consul Hewett had signed a provisional six months' treaty in 1884, and at the court of equity meeting of January 17, 1885, Vice-Consul White again got the chiefs "to sign the Treaty of Protection with Great Britain for a further period of six months ending August 1st 1885." This seems to have been the last renewal.

The Brass River court of equity referred its quarrels with other British commercial interests, such as with the National African Company at Akassa, to the consul and the naval officers. But, in the last resort, they found it more effective to fight such battles in Britain through the African Association of Liverpool, public opinion, and Parliament. The traders on the spot jockied for vantage positions by alliances with local chiefs and by the signing of "treaties."

Much of the court's time and energy, then, was taken up with political and judicial problems of arbitration of disputes, or with the maintenance or extension of trading areas. The court of equity also tackled such matters as the fixing of exchange rates of goods for palm oil, palm kernel, and the metal bar used as currency. These rates had to be "mutually agreed upon" and submitted in formal notes to the kings and chiefs of Ogbolomabiri, Bassambiri, and Twon. One such note was sent in December 1885 to "King Ebeffa of Bassambra, Chief Egbetta and his Chiefs of O'Bullambra and to Chief Cameroons, Governor of Tuwan." At that date, Ebifa was king of Bassambiri and Chief Igbeta was regent in Ogbolomabiri.

The life of the court of equity came to an end with the declaration of a Protectorate. The court, however, was only notified of the fact a year later. The court received on May 12, 1886, a copy of the West African Order-in-Council of March 26, 1885. This order had ruled "all Courts of Equity superseded by a Consular Court." Until such a consular court was established, the Brass court of equity continued its life under the name of "Court of Commerce." Regulations for the new court were drawn up by Acting Consul Harry Johnston in June 1886. He called it "a Governing Council to manage the local affairs of Brass."

GOVERNING COUNCIL

The first meeting of Acting Consul Johnston's Governing Council for Brass River was held on November 26, 1887. The council was in practice merely an official variety of the court of equity. A significant difference, however, was the addition of local chiefs as permanent members who were required to attend meetings regularly. The experiment did not find favour with the Foreign Office, and the appointment of Major Claude MacDonald as commissioner and consul-general in 1891 marked the end of this chapter in Harry Johnston's innovations.

The regulations defined the council's powers as follows:

The powers of the Council will be limited to the carrying out of Consular orders, the preservation of peace, the maintenance of highways and means of communication, the regulation of commerce and the hearing in court of minor civil actions and criminal charges.

They also set out, in detail, rates of fines, terms of imprisonment, number of lashes, and procedure for appeal to the consul. The consul was permanent president and in his absence a vice-president would preside. The council was to meet once a week and to render quarterly reports to the consul; the council later decided to meet every Friday at 4 P.M. The clerk was to be paid £25 a year, and the boys of chiefs traveling from Nembe were to be given twenty pounds of rice and three pints of rum. Chief Cameroon, who was to deliver mail for members in Nembe, was to be paid a pound for each journey.

The council was given specific duties to perform:

1. It was to seize and confiscate arms sold in contravention of the regulations "prohibiting the importation, sale or purchase of machine guns, cannon, breach loading guns, bullets, cartridges, etc."

2. The council was further to collect comey, paying half to the kings of Nembe. The other half of the comey dues was to constitute its funds "together with all court fees for expenditure in the interest of the country."

There is no evidence that the chiefs of Nembe paid greater respect to the governing council than they did to the court of equity. In May 1888, the Royal Niger Company lodged a complaint with the council. Chief Igbeta had seized four Osomari girls for a debt of 107 measures of oil and two slaves. The company was ready to pay the 107 measures of oil but not the two slaves, if Chief Igbeta returned the captured Osomari girls. When Acting Consul Johnston was informed of the matter, he instructed by telegram that Chief Igbeta be asked to return the Osomari "instanter" or in default to pay 50 puncheons and endure the visit of a gunboat. The chief was to be told that H.M.S. "Bramble" was in any case soon arriving at Brass. A letter on these lines was composed and sent to Chief Igbeta. It was returned unopened with the message that the chief was unable to read. After Johnston had threatened action similar to that taken against King Jaja of Opobo, and sent naval officers to visit him, Chief Igbeta finally returned the prisoners — about two months after the demand.

An example of "the maintenance of highways and means of communication" work of the council may be given here in conclusion. On February 24, 1888, the council awarded Townsend a contract of £160 to build a road between the white trading beaches and the town of Twon. The road was to be placed 300 yards behind the sea front, be 30 feet wide, with gutters 10 feet deep on either side.

TRUST AND CURRENCY

The European trade on the coast was based on the trust system. On arrival on the coast, a supercargo had to trust considerable amounts of manufactured goods to a local trading chief or persons recommended by him. It was the middleman's turn then to trade these goods for slaves, palm oil or kernel, ivory, or food. The name "trust" seems to have been applied originally to denote the fact of the white traders "trusting" their goods to the Delta middlemen. The goods thus trusted were in time called trusts. They were, in the second quarter of this century, called "market trust" on the Brass River — meaning goods taken from the European factory or shop (*faktiri*) for sale in the local markets. The proceeds were returned to the white man, less profits.

The trust system must have developed on the Slave Coast before 1700. William Bosman in his *New and Accurate Description of the Coast of Guinea*, published in London in 1705, says:

But if there happen to be no stock of slaves, the factor must then resolve to run the risque of trusting the inhabitants with Goods to the value of one or two hundred slaves; which commodities they send into the in-land Country, in order to buy with them slaves at all Markets. . . .

For the Delta middleman it was most convenient to be able to take goods without the need of initial capital. The possession of these European wares was further a source of prestige and an ingredient of the trade in the interior markets. When King Boy Amain brought the Lander brothers from Aboh in 1830, he had to compete with certain Bonny traders who had arrived first. He succeeded in gaining favor at Aboh not only because of his personality and cleverness, but because he had brought from the coast many more new European goods.

The white traders also became wedded to the system. It became a way of ensuring a regular supply of produce; it further ensured that rival traders did not obtain a footing where an old customer had entrenched himself by giving liberal trusts. The result often was that the chiefs were continually in debt to the white trading agents. The white agents were in fact so attached to the trust system that they disregarded warnings against it from British, as they did from local authorities. During the sixteenth meeting of the governing council on March 12, 1888, Acting Consul Johnston ruled against the giving of trusts: "On and after 10th April next any person giving out trust to the native traders, do so at their own risk, the Government will not give any assistance to obtain its repayment."

The trust system continued unabated after Johnston's declaration. Where trusts were given to persons unable to satisfy its conditions, the Houses or House heads were held responsible. In a letter dated July 20, 1888, Chief James A. Spiff wrote to the governing council warning against the giving of trusts to members of his House.

"As things are in an unsettled state presently by our not having Markets, I hereby send this for your information that on and after the 31st day of July '88, any Trusts given to any person or persons belonging to or having any connection with the House of the late Chief Thomas Spiff of Brass, that I the representative of the above named House shall on no account be answerable or responsible to any claim or claims of any merchant or trader, who is incapable of collecting such debts." The traders decided, unanimously, to ignore this timely warning.

The trust credit continued to the thirties of this century. When the government wished to repeal the House Rule Ordinance in 1912–15, it was feared that the collapse of the Houses would mean the loss to the merchants of their trust goods. The Houses didn't collapse, and they continued to serve as a means of collecting trust debts.

CURRENCY

Most of the early forms of currency used for local trade on the Niger and some parts of the Delta did not become common on the Brass River. The cowrie shell (*okoba*) apparently remained a curiosity in Nembe, and is to be found today mainly in the recesses of shrines. The Landers, indeed, reported that in 1830 Brass traders exchanged their goods by barter at Aboh, "the cowrie shell not being circulated lower down the river than Bocqua." Nor was the manilla (*anda igbogi*: bent or curved money) as important here as it was in such Delta ports as Bonny.

One of the first media of exchange used in this area would appear to have been the salt manufactured locally. Dr. Baikie gives a record of the use of salt as currency in 1854:

At Abo a great medium of barter is salt, which is brought up from Nimbe [Nembe] and from Bini [Benin], and is always in demand.

Slaves are almost always purchased with salt, the prices varying somewhat according to the condition of the market. The average price of a stout male is from ten to twelve bags of salt, or from 6,000 to 7,000 cowries, and for a good looking young female, eight to ten bags of salt, or from 4,500 cowries.[19]

Different exchange media were used for the trade with Europeans on the coast. Spanish dollars and doubloons were used in the slave trade. In 1859 the Liverpool merchant, William Cole, saw Nembe traders at Aboh "taking with them plenty of slaves" and he supposed "they managed to get rid of their living freight for doubloons." The dollar has become part of local dialect as the name for the two shilling piece.

In time, brass, copper, and iron bars were used extensively as currency. According to Barbot, the importation of these bars into the Kalabari area began in the seventeenth century: "The English and Dutch import there a great deal of copper in small bars, round and equal, about three feet long, weighing about a pound and a quarter, which the blacks of Calbary [Kalabari] work with much art, splitting the bar into three parts, from one end to the other which they polish as fine as gold, and twist the three pieces together very ingeniously like cords, to make what sort of arm rings they please." [20]

By the nineteenth century, metal bars were no longer used, but the concept of the bar was retained as a unit of reckoning: thus in Bonny Dr. Baikie reported that, in 1854, the currency was "in manillas, small horseshoe shaped pieces of copper," but accounts were kept in bars — a bar being equal to seven pence. On the Brass River there was no single currency, but accounts were kept in bars as at Bonny. Here, produce was exchanged directly for goods, designated "big cargo" and "small cargo," the value of each being computed in bars (see Appendix VIII). "Big cargo" comprised such goods as cases of Peter's gin (*jini igba*), kegs of gunpowder, guns, and demijohns. Other goods like madras, rifles, pots, etc., were classified "small cargo." The court of equity stabilized the value of the bar by fixing the rates of exchange for palm oil — "bar for oil," or for palm kernels — "bar for kernels."

In the first decade of this century, one of the "big cargo," Peter's gin, became a unit of currency. It was used in all commercial transactions, in the payment of bridewealth, and even for fines in court. Peter's gin was superseded by British money economy.

TRADE RENTS

When the supercargoes left their hulks (*olikị*) to trade on beaches, they made treaties and agreements. In Brass, the terms of occupancy were settled in the Comey (customs duty) Treaty of 1856 (Appendix III). On March 12, 1888, Acting Consul Johnston ruled that the foreshore and beaches occupied by the British merchants was to extend no more than three hundred yards and that any extension beyond this limit could only be made by arrangement with the owners.

It is not clear how long the 1856 understanding about the freedom of "ground for the erection of houses" lasted. At the twenty-fourth meeting of the governing council on May 11, 1888, Chief Kemmer wished to know what rent the Telegraph Company paid and to whom. The company explained later that what it paid "was not comey but rent, King Ebefa said the land belonged to the O'Bullambra [Ogbolomabiri] people and he had taken rent thinking it was comey. . . ." The arrangement at this time seems to have been for organizations or persons to pay comey if they engaged in trade and rent if they were not assessed for comey. This is the most likely interpretation of a query by Chief Kemmer in the governing council against the Royal Niger Company which owned three beaches at Twon. Chief Kemmer wished to know what was the status of the company as it neither traded at Brass nor paid comey, or rent in lieu of comey.

When the government of the Niger Coast Protectorate wished to make a permanent establishment, it had to prepare a deed of lease. This was done with the chiefs of Nembe on April 1, 1896. Three beaches — Elizabeth Beach, Townsend's or Cable Beach, and Custom Beach — were finally given up to the government. The 1896 deed was "for an indefinite term at a rental of £20 a year." Extensions of the ground were made between 1909–1912 and the rental was increased to £54 a year. When the native administration was set up, a part of the land was given over and by 1930 both the native administration and the government were paying £15 each. This reduced rate of rental was said to have been a result of the withdrawal of the trading firms from Brass at this period. The high court, Aba, accordingly increased the government's rent to £30 a year in 1949, on the grounds that the value of land and prices generally had increased since 1930.

An agreement for the lease of land to a trading company is reproduced at Appendix IV. Here the Brass Trading Company (John
Holt & Co.) agreed in 1899 to pay a rent of £25 a year for a beach.[21]
The beach had been occupied in turn by the Senegal Company, by
the African Direct Telegraph Company, and by Thomas Welsh and
Company. The African Direct Telegraph Company admitted in
1888 to paying rents of an unspecified amount. Its successors, and
perhaps predecessors, too, may have paid rent. It may be, however,
that after the abolition of comey in 1891 (and substitution of government subsidies) all merchants were required to pay rents.

In 1911 Chief Young Dede instituted proceedings against the African Association "for a declaration of title" for grounds it occupied
at Twon. The suit was instituted on behalf of "the house of Kulo"
and for the period the case lasted the chiefs of Nembe agreed to let
Chief Dede draw the government rents at Twon. The case ended
in the Privy Council in March 1914. The lords of the judicial com-
mittee of the Privy Council found that "the defendants and their
predecessors have been in occupation for a period prior to 1879."
Their lordships found further that a change occurred in 1891 of
whose nature they were not certain — "But it is certain that no rent
ever has been paid by a trader established under the old regime, the
only persons who did pay being the Telegraph Company, who were
not a trading Company and who made a special arrangement."
Judgment was given against Chief Young Dede, and the African
Association was exempted from the payment of rent as long as it
paid customs dues to government. This judgment may represent a
misunderstanding of the 1891 changes. Or it may mean that the
1891 changes did not in fact require old established traders to begin
to pay rent.

From Comey to Subsidy

Nothing shows more clearly the shifting of authority resulting
from the arrival of the British than the changes that gradually over-
took the payment of comey to the coastal chiefs. When British traders
first arrived to trade in palm oil and kernel, they had to rely on the
local rulers for protection. Those same chiefs and rulers were responsible for bringing down the produce from the hinterland. The traders
needed their good will. Even after British consuls had been established for the Bights of Benin and Biafra in 1849, the consul could

do no more than serve as a liaison between the rulers and the traders. The consuls arranged good-will treaties and pacts intended to foster and regulate trade. The traders on their part found it politic to make a number of payments to the rulers of the rivers they traded at. A trader had to give a "shake-hand" or present to the king and chiefs he traded with on each voyage. He would also be expected to make "dashes" to the king and his friends. The most important imposition however, was the "comey," which was an official duty which a trader had to pay to the ruler before he was allowed to do business.

The origin of the word comey is uncertain, but it may have been derived from the Portuguese word *comer*, meaning, "to eat." The Portuguese may have used this term as an equivalent of the local expression for exacting a fee or imposing a duty.

An old coast trader has described the usual formalities that were observed at the payment of comey.[22] The king would arrive at the trader's hulk or ship with his chiefs, priest, and upwards of forty canoe men. As the king and his chiefs mounted the gangway ladder, a libation of spirit or palm wine was poured first by the priest and then by the king. The trader then escorted the party to the dining room. A repast of pickled pork, salt beef, tinned salmon, cabin biscuits, roast fowls and goat, and vegetables would have been got ready. At the end of this course, port wine would be produced for the ruler, beer or gin for the chiefs. It was after this dining and wining that the comey was paid—normally a settled sum. The trader would, however, need to give further presents to both the king, his chiefs, and his canoe boys. When this business was over, the trader fired six or seven guns to show that trade could now start. An equal number was fired at the close of business. Conversely, the "breaking" of trade could be announced by the king sending off the first canoe of produce to the ship, and by his sending a messenger around with the news.

COMEY RULES AND REGULATIONS ON THE BRASS RIVER

There is no evidence that the chiefs and people of Nembe entered into any formal comey arrangement with the merchants on the Brass River before 1856. King Boy Amain's treaty with Nicolls in 1834 may have had commercial provisions, but it was called a "Treaty Offensive and Defensive" and appears to have been related solely to the slave trade.[23]

According to tradition, King Forday Kulo of Ogbolomabiri and Mein of Bassambiri were the first on the Brass River to receive comey. The year 1822 has been mentioned as the date on which King Forday Kulo received legitimate traders into the River. In 1830, however, King Kulo demanded a "book" (check or bill) of four bars from the Landers. The king declared this amount to be a customary duty he charged all white men who came to the river. The Landers also recorded of King Jacket Mein that he would "permit no foreigners whatever to pass up or down the Niger without exacting the accustomed fees or duties."

On November 17, 1856, a comey agreement was signed between the "chiefs and people of Brass and Her Britannic Majesty's Consul for the Bight of Biafra." The articles of this treaty were to "be the laws existing between the British supercargoes and the natives for the regulation of trade matters" and were to be observed by all.

Article 1 declared that the kings and chiefs had agreed to give up slave trading in appreciation of "the benefit of legitimate traffic." It is, however, neither stated nor implied that the slave trade was to be given up because comey was going to be paid, or that comey was to be a price for the abandonment of the slave trade. The comey rules and regulations were simply an attempt to systematize something that already existed. The rules were as follows:

1. Trading vessels were to pay comey according to their size: "vessels of two masts to pay two puncheons worth of goods; vessels of three masts to pay three puncheons worth of goods to each king (Kiya of Obullambry and Arishma of Bassambry)," i.e., Kien of Ogbolomabiri and Arisimo of Bassambiri.[24]
2. If vessels merely carried cargo into the river and did not carry out produce for export, no comey was to be charged.
3. If vessels did not complete lading in the Brass River but had to go elsewhere to complete the task, the comey was to be five bars for each cask.

The rights and privileges the British supercargoes had to gain for the payment of comey were enumerated in Article 7:

1. The only other fee they could be charged apart from the comey was to be for pilotage: "no other tax or payment is to be made under any pretence whatever."
2. The traders were to be given watering facilities free of charge "in the pilots' Town called Twaw" [Twon].

3. "Ground for the erection of houses and for the storing of casks and goods" was "to be granted free of all charges." The British occupants of such land were also authorized to consider it "British property" and so to maintain their "right of occupancy."

A copy of the treaty was, finally, to be furnished to each of the chiefs, who were to produce it when demanding comey. The portion on pilotage was also to be copied out and given to the chief pilot, who would similarly give it to masters of vessels entering the river.

The first amendment of the 1856 arrangements came in the treaty dated December 3, 1879, between the chiefs and the British traders and approved by the consul for the Bight of Biafra at Fernando Po (S. F. Easton).

By this treaty, payment was still to be made to "two kings." [25] The rate, however, was to be "one piece of satin stripe between them for each puncheon hove," that is, the comey duty was to be levied according to the quantity of produce carried away.[26]

Britain declared the Oil Rivers Protectorate on June 5, 1885, and in March 1888 Acting Consul Harry Johnston unilaterally altered the existing comey arrangements. He issued a document, "Regulations about payment of comey in the Brass Districts," embodying his new rules: comey was to be levied as "an export duty" on palm oil, palm kernel. The consul would pay half of the proceeds to "the king of Nimbi [Nembe], and the other half will be paid to the Governing Council for expenditure in the interests of the country as stipulated in the Consul's order for the constitution of that Council."

The main change introduced by the 1888 regulations was the taking over of control of the Oil Rivers Protectorate by the government. The rulers of Nembe were to receive only half of the proceeds of comey from the new authority and under no circumstances directly from the traders. The consul no longer restricted himself to mediating between trader and local ruler in the formulation of comey rules, but made such rules and undertook to administer them. This change was a sign of the changing times — a sign that the British government was taking direct responsibility for the protection of British commercial interests and that it was more and more taking over authority from the rulers of the Delta states. The take-over was, however, not yet complete: the proceeds were divided, symbolically, half and half.

In 1891, Sir Claude MacDonald, commissioner and consul-general of the Niger Coast Protectorate, introduced further changes. In a dispatch of June 11, 1891, he enumerated new regulations that were to operate in all the rivers from August 1, 1891. Comey was officially defined as being originally payments made to chiefs for their good offices in promoting European trade. These payments to the chiefs were now finally "abolished." The government, however, undertook to make compensatory payments to be called "subsidies." The government intended raising the money for the purpose by imposing customs duties "for the benefit of the country, and in the name of the various chiefs, the revenue being devoted to the payment of subsidies, in lieu of 'Comey,' the expenses of Administration and to the opening up and development of the country generally."

Sir Claude MacDonald adopted the novel procedure of going from one river to another to obtain the express consent of the chiefs to his new arrangements — especially on the imposition of customs duties. The Nembe chiefs signed the document, reluctantly, on the condition that the commissioner would do something about the new trade monopoly instituted by the Royal Niger Company at Akassa.[27]

After comey became subsidy paid by the government, both its origin and purpose became confused. The time came when even the government lost sight of the purpose for which subsidy was paid. Some "comey subsidies" or "subsidies of comey origin" became indistinguishable from subsidies paid by government to certain chiefs for services rendered or for other causes than as compensation for comey fees. It was in such circumstances that the African Association claimed that beaches it occupied at Twon had been handed to them by King Koko in 1891 on the basis of a payment by the company of comey to the King.[28]

When even the purpose of comey subsidies became obscured, government officials became less and less able to support their continued payment. Some subsidies remained in abeyance over years until resuscitated by new claimants, others became the subject of prolonged litigation between two or more rivals. Government officials began to take the view that the chiefs currently receiving comey subsidies no longer carried out any public duties to justify the payment to them personally of such subsidies. It was recognized that the rightful heirs to the original comey dues were the entire communities and not merely the individual descendants of the chiefs. The "Comey Subsidies Law, 1955" [29] was accordingly passed by the Legislature of Eastern Nigeria, "for the payment of Annual Grants in substitution for Comey Subsidies." From July 1, 1955, annual grants were to be paid to towns holding comey treaties, or rather "to the authorities having jurisdiction over the area in which the said towns are situated . . . to be applied for the benefit of the inhabitants thereof." Persons currently in receipt of comey subsidies were allowed to continue for their lifetime.

Comey has thus changed from a trade tax to, first, a quarterly government subsidy payable to individual chiefs, and finally to a government annual grant to native authorities or local government bodies to be applied for the benefit of entire communities. The changes reflect the various changes that have occurred in the balance of power as between British and indigenous rulers, as between traditional authorities and the people, in the period from 1856 to 1955.

Non-Comey Subsidies

In 1891 Sir Claude MacDonald had decided to pay government subsidies to chiefs already receiving comey. It would appear to have been a way of winning and retaining the support of influential chiefs. Both the government of the Niger Coast Protectorate and of the Protectorate of Southern Nigeria exploited the strategy of subsidies in their bid to gain the loyalty of chiefs or to win them from evil courses. It was these later subsidies, granted solely on the volition of government, that came to complicate claims for comey subsidies. The government came to take the view that it was only obliged to continue the payment of subsidies derived from comey, and that all other subsidies ceased with the death of the original recipient. All subsidies paid to chiefs in Okrika, Owerri, Awo, Oguta, and on the River Nun were of non-comey origin. There were a number of subsidies paid in the Nembe area, too, which were not of comey origin. [30]

Okpoma Subsidy. There are no clear records to determine the origin of the Okpoma subsidy, but a plausible account runs as follows. Once upon a time Chief Sagbe Obasi — who later became king of Okpoma — lived with Chief Kalango at Bassambiri. Civil strife broke out between the Mein and Kalango Houses of Bassambiri, in which Chief Obasi lost much property. He returned to Okpoma and threatened hostilities against Kalango if he was not compensated for his losses. Chief Obasi died before the quarrel could be settled. His nephew, Obu, who also was amanyanabo of Okpoma, took up the quarrel. The government of the Niger Coast Protectorate would have none of this bickering, and paid Obu a subsidy of £30 to keep the peace.

After Obu's death, a subsidy of £20 was paid each year to the head of the Obasi House. In 1933 a dispute arose between Chief Willie K. Obasi,[31] head of the Obasi House, and Chief R. O. Tubu, amanyanabo of Okpoma, over who was entitled to receive the subsidy. It was claimed that the subsidy was, in fact, part of the comey paid to Koko and Ebifa, and was, accordingly, payable to the amanyanabo of Okpoma and not to the head of Obasi House. Sir Claude MacDonald's declaration on the occasion of its first payment gives no decisive clue. The money was paid to Obu "to look after his town and maintain its good behaviour." The government finally ruled this subsidy to be of non-comey origin, and not open to revival.

Ewoama Subsidy. In the 1890's Chief Digiboerigha was obliged by a feud in Okpoma to break away to found the town of Ewoama (New Town). Ten out of the thirty pounds subsidy paid to Obu of Okpoma was transferred to the amanyanabo of Ewoama. Digiboerigha's successor as amanyanabo of Ewoama, Chief Abayeh, received the annual subsidy of ten pounds until his death in November 1914. Thereafter a succession dispute broke out, and in 1939 the government declared the Ewoama subsidy, along with that of Okpoma, not of comey origin.

Twon Subsidy. There are two isolated records of subsidies paid to chiefs of Twon, but their origin is unknown. A subsidy of twelve pounds a year was paid to Chief Uriah Cameron from 1910 to 1915. This was stopped by the commissioner for Warri Province in 1915.[32] No reason was given. Another chief, George, also received a subsidy of six pounds from 1915–20.

In the third schedule to the Comey Subsidies Law 1955, the grants payable to the Nembe native administration were to be applied for the benefit of the inhabitants of Nembe and Twon. The inclusion of Twon must have been due to the fact that Twon was mentioned in the 1856 Treaty as a place where the traders would be given watering facilities and provided with pilots. All comey had, in fact,

King Francis Osamade Joseph Allagoa, Mingi X,
the present king of Nembe, who has ruled since 1954

His Highness, the Reverend Anthony O. Ockiya, Mingi IX,
who ruled from 1926 to 1936

King Frederick William Koko, Mingi VIII (1889–1898),
who was the prosecutor of the Akassa War

gone directly to the amanyanabo of Nembe; Twon had never been a sharer of comey.

House Subsidies. King Ebifa (1870–94) of Bassambiri and King Koko (1889–98) of Ogbolomabiri were the last to receive comey subsidies as holders of the office of amanyanabo in Nembe. The amounts paid are easy to check after 1888.[33] After August 1, 1891, the government paid a fixed annual sum of thirty pounds to each of the amanyanabo in lieu of comey. After the raid by King Koko and the Nembe people on the Royal Niger Company at Akassa in 1895, the government appointed a council of six House heads with whom it would deal in place of the king. These chiefs were "chosen for their personality and assistance at the enquiry which was held after the raid," and to them was paid the comey subsidy originally paid to Kings Ebifa and Koko.

The six chiefs chosen in 1895 to receive comey continued to receive a payment of ten pounds each per annum during their lifetime, which was transmitted to their successors in office as House head. The subsidies became the property of the Houses of the six chiefs. As the original payments had been to both kings of Ogbolomabiri and Bassambiri, three chiefs from each quarter were selected: Chiefs Nathaniel Yekorogha (Hardstone) of Yekorogha House, Edmund Natebo of Kien House (a branch of Amain House), and Thomas Ockiya of Ockiya House from Ogbolomabiri; Chiefs Christopher Warri of Warri House, Smoke Amabebe of Pegi House, and Kalango of Epemu House from Bassambiri.

The balance between the two quarters was destroyed when, in 1905, the government authorized the payment of a further ten pounds to each of three Ogbolomabiri chiefs: Edward Nanyo of Yemainain House, Fatewari of Iboama House, and Kponi Igbeta of Igbeta House (a branch of Iboama House). The additional total of thirty pounds for chiefs in Nembe was paid by the government to correct the difference between the sixty pounds then paid at Nembe and the five hundred pounds paid to chiefs at Opobo.

The total sum of subsidies paid to chiefs in Nembe remained at ninety pounds until 1910. In that year the payment to Chief Nathaniel Yekorogha was increased by two pounds "because the Nembe Council met in his house or compound and because of his particular services to Government."[34]

The ten-pound House subsidies continued to be drawn by the heads of the original Houses until the 1955 law. In a few Houses, however, the subsidy passed into the hands of heads of branches of the main House. Disputes arose as a result in some cases, and the payments were recovered by the original line of chiefs. In other cases, the right of collecting comey subsidies passed permanently into the hands of the new claimant's House.[35]

6

THE NINETEENTH CENTURY

The nineteenth century was a fateful period in which European contact wrought changes, either by direct impact or by indirect effect. It is also a period for which evidence is more plentiful.

KINGS KULO AND MEIN

The first decades of the nineteenth century saw two remarkable rulers — King Forday Kulo (1800–32) on the throne of Ogbolomabiri, and King Jacket Mein on the Bassambiri throne.

Both the Landers and Laird and Oldfield (1832) saw King Forday Kulo, then an old king who had handed affairs of state to his son King Boy Amain. The Landers described King Kulo, who conversed with them "in tolerably good English," as he was in 1830:

King Forday is a complacent, venerable-looking old man — his fondness for spirituous liquors is extreme, and he drank large potations of it in our presence, though it produced no visible effect either upon his manners or conversation.[1]

Oldfield saw King Kulo before his death in 1832, and he confirms the king's addiction to liquor: "King Forday is a very old man, and very much addicted to rum." [2] Kulo had, however, not been an old drinking man all his life. He had been an effective ruler, and Tepowa says of him that "he was the most famous and popular among Nembe kings. . . . King Kulo invited the Europeans from Akassa to trade in Brass, as it was their nearest trading port . . . the name of King Kulo will ever be remembered by the towns-people, for in his days they ceased to be sold as slaves." [3]

King Jacket Mein was a completely different character. None of the explorers recorded a meeting with him, but he had the reputation for being a fiery and predatory chief. The Landers recorded that King Jacket Mein claimed sovereignty over the route to the Niger and would let no foreigners in without exacting fees, and that the king was "a noted scoundrel." [4] Oldfield, who visited Nembe in 1832, also stayed at Ogbolomabiri with King Boy Amain and Kulo, but ascribed great power to King Jacket, who possessed "the most absolute authority." [5]

The Reverend D. O. Ockiya's account of Mein's life shows something of his ruthlessness. Mein's mother, Ina of Ekpetiama or Tombia, was first married to King Ogbodo by "big dowry" but had no children with him. After Ogbodo's death she was married to Chief Opo of Ogbolomabiri. She called her son Mein (which means the opposite bank, the crossing). She recrossed to Bassambiri when Opo died, and the boy Mein grew up among the sons of Ogbodo. These young men, however, became jealous of Mein's abilities, and sold him to King Opubo of Bonny. [6] It was here in Bonny that Mein got his habit of wearing jackets and was nicknamed King Jacket by the supercargoes.

Ina returned to Ekpetiama in sorrow. Her brother Feingha, however, obtained from a medicine man a magic mat and blanket. These articles he sent by two small boys with a supply of palm produce through Nembe to Bonny. The messengers were enjoined to deliver the mat and blanket without speaking to anyone. This they did. The result was that Mein, after using the mat and blanket, succeeded in persuading King Opubo to let him go. The necessary redemption fee was paid out of the proceeds of the sale of the palm produce. Mein lived in Ekpetiama for some time and then returned to Bassambiri as a trader.

Ogbodo's children were completely taken in by Mein's simulation of friendship. He gave one of them a woman slave to serve in sweeping Ogbodo's tomb. This woman went mad and finally disappeared. This put the ruler in debt to Mein. He also paid the debts of another ruler, and did so on the condition that the Bassambiri throne revert to him and his descendants forever.

As king of Bassambiri, Mein was a great upholder of the rights of his dynasty against the claims of the Ogbolomabiri kings. He fought a sanguinary engagement against King Kulo at Kiberi Creek. It is related that the slaughter was so terrible that relatives of the dead could not identify the corpses except by the clothes they wore or by marks on their bodies.

This battle may have been the basis of King Jacket's awesome reputation for absolute authority. The reason given for the Kiberi war is that Ogbolomabiri war canoes used a drum, *igodogo*, to which Mein claimed sole rights.

KING BOY AMAIN (1832–46)

King Boy Amain is the best-documented king of Nembe. He is especially noted for his part in aiding Richard and John Lander in the discovery of the Delta as the mouths of the Niger in 1830. King Boy had to pay a ransom of twenty slaves to King Obie of Aboh to obtain custody of the explorers, whom he brought in his trade canoe to Nembe and to the coast at Akassa. The Landers have told the whole detailed story of their encounter with King Boy Amain in the published journal of their travels. All other Niger explorers up to 1841 give accounts of King Boy's activities up the river from the Nun entrance to Aboh.

King Boy had demanded a remuneration from the Landers, in addition to the twenty slaves he paid, of goods to "the value of fifteen bars or slaves — and likewise a cask of rum. . . ." [7] This was not paid at the time, but King Boy later found the Lander journal and handed it back to Captain Townson. The Captain claimed in 1832 to have paid the price of eight puncheons, while King Boy claimed to have received only "the price of three puncheons." [8] Richard Lander on this later occasion made the king presents of "Fifteen or sixteen guns, two barrels of gunpowder, fifteen soldiers' canteens, knives, spoons, and soldiers' coats, with various other articles." [9]

It is clear from these accounts that King Boy was the most active trading chief between the Nun-Brass estuaries and Aboh. In 1830 the Landers described his trading canoe to be of immense size, drawing four and a half feet of water and measuring over fifty feet. It carried over sixty persons and

a number of large boxes or chests which are filled with spirituous liquors, cotton, and silk goods, earthenware, and other articles of European and other foreign manufactures; besides abundance of provisions for present consumption, and two thousand yams for the master of a Spanish slaver, which is now lying in Brass river.[10]

By 1841, another explorer reported that:

The King of Brass has eighteen large canoes, with forty men in each, which he sends to Aboh for palm oil, yams, fruits, bullocks, goats, sheep, rice, and black beans, in exchange for which, he gives rum, cowries, clothes, shirts, hats, caps, knives, looking-glasses, snuff-boxes, hooks and lines, scissors, muskets, powder and ball, tumblers, wine-glasses, etc.[11]

King Boy Amain gloried in his wealth and power, and he was thought to be vain by Lander and other explorers who knew him. His bragging often created a reaction, and when in 1841 King Boy's envoys asserted that "King Boy pass all black man," that is, that King Boy was the most powerful black ruler, Allen and Thompson commented that he was, in fact, "tributary to Obi Ossai of Aboh." [12] But this was untrue. The relationship between King Boy and Obi was merely the commercial one between the middleman and the primary producer. When taxed with obsequious behaviour in 1832, King Boy had explained the position in simple terms: "King Obie too much palm-oil, King Boy too little." [13]

The truth is that King Boy used all means to get what he wanted. In 1830 Richard Lander reported that King Boy's influence at Aboh was the result of the goods he brought from the coast and the number of retainers he had with him: he had over a hundred men. He was also married to Addizetta, "Obie's favourite daughter." [14] Apparently, when King Boy went to the coast, Addizetta stayed behind to accumulate produce at Aboh and to maintain good relations for her husband.

Far from King Boy being "tributary" to Obi, the relationship between the two, between the coastal and interior peoples, was one of interdependence. This relationship was clearly shown in the account of hostile incidents between Nembe and Aboh recorded by Dr. Baikie in 1854. Obi had tried to embroil King Boy with the British by accusing him, in front of British officers, of murdering an Englishman. This was in 1842. King Boy had to leave in a hurry. From that date no more Brass trading canoes went to Aboh. But three years before Baikie's visit, King Boy had found it necessary to send a trading expedition to Aboh:

A quarrel, however, soon took place, which ended in the Abo people seizing the cargoes, and the Nimbe [Nembe] men retreating and carrying off some Abo canoes. Since then friendly relations have been dropped, but a year before the arrival of the "Pleiad" [Dr. Baikie's ship], two headmen had been dispatched to go to Nimbe to try and settle differences. But various diplomatic difficulties and delays had occurred, and when I heard the story, the Aboh envoys were still at the court of Nimbe.[15]

This episode shows that after a period of boycott both parties were forced to make a gesture of reconciliation. King Boy did so by sending trading canoes, Obie by making diplomatic moves to end the quarrel.

King Boy fought another war against the Ogbia town of Anyama before his death in 1846. According to Mr. Ockiya, the town of Egbedeama and most of the surrounding Ogbia towns supported Anyama. As the Nembe fleet approached Anyama, King Amain called a halt while he prayed and poured libations to the gods. The enemy attacked at this moment and the king was hit on the lip. Many others were killed or injured. According to Tepowa, the king, too, died from the wound later.[16] Anyama was sacked and burned, but the fleet was again ambushed on its way home.

King Boy, then, was an active merchant prince who took pride in the power wealth conferred. But he was also a man who scrupulously observed all the traditional religious rites and ceremonies of his people. Tepowa gives emphasis to this aspect of the king's character, and the Landers confirm it in their account of the journey they made with him from Aboh to Nembe in 1830. The king never ate a meal without first making a meat and drink offering. And on his arrival home, he had first to call at Oromabiri to confer with the high priest and perform necessary rites.[17]

KING KIEN (1846–63)

King Kien was the next powerful ruler to emerge following a period of succession disputes after the death of King Boy Amain. Kuki, son of King Boy Amain by Addizetta, died within a year after he had been named to succeed his father. Then Amange, a grandson of King Forday Kulo, was considered together with Kien. The matter was brought to the high priest at Oromabiri, but he suggested a deputation to the oracle at Arochuku. Thomas Hutchinson arrived in Nembe soon after this deputation had returned from Arochuku and Kien had been crowned:

Keya [Kien], the King of the Obullam Abry [Ogbolomabiri] side of Brass river, was known to have recently paid a visit there [Arochuku] to ascertain whether he or a powerful chief, named Amanga [Amange], was to be the head man.

On his return a number of the "god country" [Aro] people came with him, and lived at his place, on the fat of the land, whilst they were deliberating. Amanga, of course, was now and then present at the festivals; but one morning he became very sick, and was dead in a few hours afterwards.[18]

King Kien has the reputation of being a cruel king. Chiefs feared him for his merciless punishment of all offenders, and all adulterous wives and their partners were invariably drowned by him. He would appear thereafter for seven days in costly raiment before an assembly of the people, where the relatives of the offenders had to give presents to him in appreciation of his summary dispensation of justice. It was an offense punishable by death for any one to pass before him from left to right.

KING OCKIYA (1863–79)

In the first years of his reign, King Ockiya was able to win the love of his subjects by his qualities of daring leadership in war and humility in peacetime. The comey treaty had been signed by his predecessor in 1856 and King Ockiya ably continued the policy of friendship with the British, but he was also firm in protecting the rights of local merchants against the supercargoes. King Ockiya had invited Christian missionaries to Twon in 1864, but it was in the last decade of his reign, when he permitted them to come to Nembe and himself took baptism and the names of Josiah Constantine, that he saw the full effect of a force for division and civil strife.

King Ockiya is mainly remembered, however, for the wars he fought against neighboring peoples. The Kalabari and Otuan wars were proof to the peoples to the east and west that the kingdom of Nembe was able to defend its claims. These wars also represented the kingdom's entry into the power politics of the Delta.

The Kalabari War was caused by rivalry for trade on the Engenni and Orashi rivers in the upper Delta. The immediate cause was the piratical attack of Chief Bugo of Bassambiri on certain Kalabari men.[19] Thereupon King Abbey Amachree of Kalabari sent men to the Engenni, Orashi, and Kolo creeks with orders to seize any Nembe traders they might find. The news of this expedition, however, traveled ahead, and the Nembe traders were able to escape.

King Abbey next approached the people of Kula to act on his side. Kula accepted the bribe and served the Kalabari cause in two ways. First, they came by night and kidnapped a slave boy, Oluku, who was sleeping in his master's canoe on the Nembe waterfront. An elderly man, Igoinwari, who was also in the canoe, escaped with a deep matchet cut on his neck. He raised the alarm and canoes were launched in pursuit of the marauders. They are suspected of having hidden in a creek adjacent to the "bad bush" of Okipiri. At the time, no one would dare touch even the leaves of a tree on that piece of bush, and nobody thought of looking there. King Abbey Amachree is said to have executed his captive.

The Kula also served as spies for Kalabari and fired warning shots whenever the Nembe fleet left home waters.

Only one encounter is recorded in this war — and that a night melee. A spy observed the enemy lurking in an arm of the river and the king ordered an advance. King Ockiya's war canoe rammed an enemy canoe in the darkness and sank it. Fire was exchanged with heavy losses on both sides.

The war was practically a stalemate, but King Amachree came to Twon to sign peace arrangements conducted by the British consul, Hopkins (1871?). The west bank of the Engenni-Orashi up to Oguta was awarded to Nembe and the east bank to King Amachree. King Abbey Amachree's desire for peace was influenced by the fact that he was then at war with Bonny as well. It has, in fact, been suggested that the Nembe attack had been instigated by Bonny.[20]

King Ockiya was assisted in this war by King Arisimo of Bassambiri and later by Ebifa, who succeeded Arisimo in 1870. Among the Ogbolomabiri chiefs, Oruwari has been cited as the king's "bull dog" or leader of the war council.

The king went from the Kalabari war straight into a punitive expedition against the Ogbia town of Amadugoama. A pirate from this place, Adubonimi, had murdered Akpana, a son of Kulo, who had gone to collect a debt. Only a handful of chiefs was required to sack the town, and the murderer eventually gave himself up.

The Otuan war was a more serious affair, although its cause is not remembered. It was probably undertaken as a reprisal for some act of piracy committed on Nembe trading canoes. The provocation must have been great, because the normal practice of taking the enemy by surprise night attack was abandoned. Tepowa writes of this war that "both the King and Chiefs sacked the towns, burning up everything, so that not a vestige was left." [21]

It may have been the memory of this attack which led the Otuan chiefs to sign a treaty with the National African Company (later Royal Niger Company) on November 6, 1886, ceding to the company "for ever the whole of our territory extending from Amasoma to Angiama on either side of the creek, bounded on East by Owako-rogar and Ekebiri and on West by Osiamah." For this the company was to "protect the said chiefs from the attacks of any neighbouring aggressive tribes," and to pay the chiefs "ten measures per annum native value." [22] The Nembe people may have been among the "neighbouring aggressive tribes" of this treaty.

King Koko (1889–98)

Frederick William Koko was the last king of the century. He had been a Christian before his coronation, but he came to detest all the innovations of the white man. He publicly renounced Christianity and became the rallying point for the opposition to the new order that was creeping in with Christianity, trade, and the British consul. Opposition to the new forces came to be focused on the Royal Niger Company at Akassa, and the story of King Koko's heroic fight is told in the following chapter.

It may be noted that with the increase of external wars and commitments, the internal hostilities between Ogbolomabiri and Bassambiri virtually disappear. The Bassambiri kings generally cooperated with the kings of Ogbolomabiri in their external wars. King Ebifa (1870–94) thought so much in terms of unity that when an attempt was made to set up a Roman Catholic Mission at Bassambiri, after the Church Missionary Society was already established in Ogbolomabiri, he rejected the idea with the argument that one church was enough for Nembe.

7

THE AKASSA WAR

The story of the European trade on the Brass River told in Chapter V forms the background to the affair of 1895. The early Portuguese, Spanish, and Dutch trade in slaves had been carried on through the ports of New Calabar and Bonny. It shifted to Nembe (Brass town) when the British preventive activities became effective at these ports. When the Landers arrived in 1830, the slaving ships and baracoons were still in evidence. By 1856, the British authorities had succeeded in proving their point — legitimate trade was now more profitable than the illegitimate traffic in slaves. The Comey Treaty of that year provided for the discontinuance of the slave trade and the provision of facilities at the sea coast town of Twon for British legitimate traders. In a few years the beaches of this town on the Brass estuary had become dotted with the "factories" of the British supercargoes. By the 1860's, the Brass River had become a significant area in the Oil Rivers territory.

In the following two decades the kings and chiefs of Brass had to restrain the Liverpool merchants from their attempts to obtain produce direct from the hinterland producers. In the 1880's, after the arrival of Sir George Tubman Goldie's National African Company (which became the Royal Niger Company, Chartered and Limited, in 1886), the established supercargoes and the Nembe traders became allies against the common rival, and Liverpool merchants with stations on the Brass River agitated in the British press and Parliament against the increasingly intolerable monopoly maintained by the Niger Company at Akassa over all the markets in the interior.[1]

The proceedings of the Brass River court of equity for these years show the resentment felt by the supercargoes and the chiefs alike. On November 7, 1885, the court sent a joint letter of protest to the Liverpool African Association. On December 1, a similar letter was sent to "the Senior Officer on the Coast." These letters and petitions to British officials on the spot and in Britain continued and the British government decided to send Major Claude MacDonald as commissioner to the Niger and Oil Rivers in 1889.

When Major MacDonald visited Brass in April 1889, he received a letter from Mr. A. A. Whitehouse "as representing the European traders in the river,"[2] and another from Chief Spiff on behalf of the people of Nembe. This petition was submitted jointly by all the chiefs of Ogbolomabiri, Bassambiri, Twon, and Okpoma, and bore the names of King Ebifa of Bassambiri, King Frederick William Koko of Ogbolomabiri, King Obu of Okpoma (Fishtown), Chief Jacob Cameron, and Chief Digiboerigha (who became the first amanyanabo of Ewoama). It was thus backed by all sections of the community.

The two petitions were equally critical of the monopoly and power of the Royal Niger Company at Akassa. Whitehouse and the other traders complained against the Niger Company's customs regulations, the judicial powers exercised by that company, and the practice of the company's district agents in confiscating canoes they met on the Niger, citing a recent case of a canoe "in charge of Alligore, a well known Brass Chief" [Chief Joseph Alagoa] seized at Asaba. The commissioner concluded:

"There is no doubt that the Brass traders drew their oil supply from places which lie within the Niger Territories, and which are now closed to them. . . ."

It was his view that the Royal Niger Company need not discriminate against indigenous traders, but should treat "all the Oil Rivers natives" as "natives" in the sense of the royal charter.

In the years 1890–93, the African Association of Liverpool worked to curb the power of the Royal Niger Company by sponsoring rival companies to trade in the Niger territories, trying to force up prices there, and encouraging smuggling by the Nembe middlemen. Sir

George Goldie counterattacked vigorously by forbidding the sale of liquor above Abutshi — thus cutting off the only currency used by his rivals — raising the duty on palm oil, buying off the competing firms, and making stricter arrangements for warding off smugglers. In June 1893, Goldie succeeded in buying off the African Association itself, which promised to "stay away from the Niger" and to "stop all its public criticism of the Niger Company." [3]

By 1893, therefore, the chiefs of Nembe had lost their most effective ally and were faced with more stringent regulations and checks. The year 1894 was the company's year, with no European competitors and an efficient system of control against smuggling.

If, by the beginning of 1894, the traders of the Brass district had no hope of aid from the white traders, it was equally clear to them that no redress could be got through appeals to consuls. The long story of futile negotiations with British government agents is told in Annex C to the Kirk Report, "Case of the Brass Chiefs." In 1878, Consul D. Hopkins had offered them the markets from Aboh to the sea. In 1884, Consul Edward Hyde Hewett arrived to sign a treaty, but the chiefs insisted that some assurance be given on the question of markets. Hewett dodged the issue by persuading them to sign a mere interim treaty for six months. In January 1885, Vice-Consul H. A. White returned to renew the treaty up to August 1, 1885, and a further promise of consultation with the home government was used to secure signature. When Hewett returned in March 1886, he announced that the question of markets could no longer be discussed. as the government had decided "that markets could not be divided nor given to any one particularly, that white men and black men might trade equally in all markets. . . ." After the chiefs had agreed to free trade, however, Consul Hewett returned to announce the grant of a royal charter to the National African Company which then became the Royal Niger Company, Chartered and Limited.

This situation, of course, led to the further protests to MacDonald in 1889 and in 1891 when he returned to establish the government of the Niger Coast Protectorate. MacDonald promised a vice-consul for Brass to look after the chiefs' interests. From 1891 such a vice-consul was appointed and yet, up to the end of 1894, no improvement had occurred; things had, in fact, gone from bad to worse. On his last visit before the attack, the consul declared that there was "nothing to do on the Niger Company's matter again." [4]

In these circumstances there was a strong temptation for the chiefs to resort to war. Unfortunately, the company allowed itself to carry out provocative acts. A ship, the "Masaba," was moored on the Ekole Creek (Onitoru), along which the Nembe people had to pass through to the Niger. This ship fired on canoes whether they were carrying trade goods (i.e., smuggling) or merely carrying foodstuff. People were killed and wounded in these affrays, and the abandoned canoes, with their contents, were then confiscated.

The company also sent round to the Ijaw and other immediate neighbors of Nembe, ordering them not to pay any debts owed to Nembe men. The company's representative agreed at the Kirk enquiry that the company did not recognize "trust debts." This order had indeed been embodied in Regulation XXVIII, the "Debt Regulation," later called the "Protection of Natives Regulation." The effect was to prevent persons from outside the company's territory from collecting debts owed to them.

It is evident, too, that certain company servants taunted the people and treated them brutally, telling them that they would be forced to eat dust. An allegation was made against a Captain Christian, who ordered a woman to be stripped naked and covered with tar. Such taunts and brutalities, the chiefs declared, made them vow "to die by their [the company's] guns instead of hunger." [5]

The timing of the attack was dictated, also, by internal conditions. From 1879 to 1889, Ogbolomabiri was without an amanyanabo and accordingly the largest unit of the clan had been without leadership. There was the amanyanabo of Bassambiri, King Ebifa (1870–94), but he was essentially a man of peace, and when King Frederick William Koko arrived on the scene, King Ebifa served merely to restrain him. Chief Igbeta was the most outstanding personality at this period, but he refused to be crowned king. Proof of this tradition exists in the proceedings of the court of equity for Brass River. On March 12, 1888, Acting Consul Johnston asked Chief Igbeta to receive "one quarter share of the whole comey but Egbeta objected saying he was not King." The money he refused was used to defray outstanding debts of King Ockiya. Chief Igbeta is said to have died on November 19, 1888, and Koko was made king early the following year. From this time until the death of Ebifa in November 1894, there were two heads to reason things out. From November 1894 to January 29, 1895, King Koko was sole commander-in-chief. He had strong-minded chiefs as lieutenants and advisers, but his was the prerogative to issue the orders, and when he ordered an attack on the Akassa depot of the Royal Niger Company on January 29, 1895, the whole people went with him.

NATURE OF THE WAR

British political agents and officials of the Royal Niger Company have labeled the campaign as the Akassa Raid. Later scholars have tended to think of it as no more than a raid. In the British view, the attack on Akassa on the morning of Tuesday, January 29, 1895, was the central event in the whole affair. The British thenceforward looked at all succeeding events in the light of what happened on that morning.

The empire builders of the day were, moveover, incapable of considering any passage of arms with a subject or near-subject people as anything more than a "disturbance." Sir John Kirk, who was sent to enquire into the matter, submitted a report on "the disturbances at Brass." In the report he referred to "the recent outrages committed by the people of Brass." Even Sir Claude MacDonald, the Commissioner and Consul-General of the Niger Coast Protectorate, who was more sympathetic than most, in his despatches repeatedly referred to what happened as a raid and an outrage. Officials of the Royal Niger Company, of course, pressed home this interpretation of the incident. To them, it was the wild unprovoked act of savages. According to the company, the complaints and protests made by the people were made up by persons (white men) hostile to it. In their view, even the damage done to machinery during the attack on Akassa could not have been encompassed by the "natives" on their own.

Local historians, on the other hand, invariably speak of "the Akassa War" (*Akassa Youmi*). They describe a campaign beginning with the raid on the Niger Company's depot on January 29 through the punitive attacks on Nembe and Okpoma in the following month, and culminating in the Kirk Commission of Inquiry. During all this period, there was a state of war. The people could not come out of hiding or ply freely in the rivers, and the launches of the Royal Niger Company were burning any villages on the banks of the main rivers suspected of supporting the Nembe people. The official reports tell the same story.

The charge of irresponsible savage outburst is unsupported by the

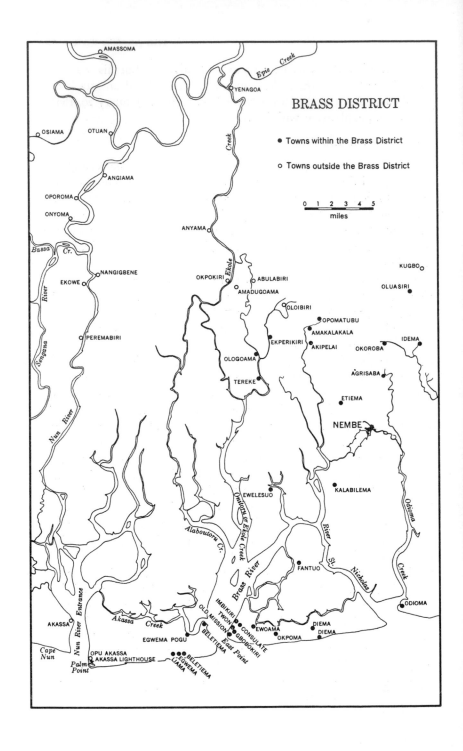

facts. It was a conflict caused by long-standing grievances made known to government and company officials for many years. When Cuthbert Harrison took over from Harper Moore as vice-consul at Brass on January 15, 1895, that officer had been told that all was well in the Brass district, and that "the only likelihood of trouble would be the question of the Niger markets now in possession of the Niger Company and at which in former times the Brassmen were allowed to trade." [6] On January 27, two days before the attack, the acting vice-consul sent on a letter of warning to Joseph Flint, the agent general of the company at Akassa. Flint's reply shows that the company was fully aware of the long standing quarrel with the people of Nembe. Flint told the new vice-consul: "these rumours are generally in evidence at this time of year but this is the first notification . . . from the Consulate in Brass." [7] The agent general was also unable to believe the warning letter because he knew several of the chiefs in person and some had visited his station recently: "chief Didi [Dede] was in Akassa a week ago yesterday and James Spiff two or three days ago."

If Joseph Flint knew some Nembe chiefs, the chiefs and people were also in a position to know the ways of the white man and the details of the machines and stores at Akassa. It would appear that some Nembe men had even been employed at the company's depot at Akassa and knew something of the working of these machines.

ATTACK ON AKASSA

At a general meeting convened by King Frederick William Koko of all the chiefs of Ogbolomabiri, Bassambiri, Twon, and Okpoma, a decision was made to throw themselves on the enemy by a surprise attack. The arrangements and the final plan of attack must have been settled between Saturday and Sunday, January 26 and 27, 1895. A Roman Catholic priest, Father Bubendorfer (or Diedenhofer) arrived at Nembe at 5 P.M. on Sundays as the guest of King Koko. The Father had brought down a son of King Koko who had been a pupil at the Society of the Holy Ghost Mission, Onitsha. Koko was apparently busy with arrangements for the raid and "he apologized for not staying longer, saying, he had to speak with other chiefs about palaver on the creeks." The Father was left in the care of the king's clerk, "John Thomas" (Eppe), and Robert Abarakasa Igbeta, "educated at a College in the Isle of Man."

At 9 P.M. of the same day (Sunday) the acting vice-consul at Twon,

Mr. C. E. Harrison, received an anonymous letter giving details of the planned attack:

> Brass people leaving tomorrow at noon to destroy Niger Company's factories and lives at Akassa on Tuesday morning, be sure you send at once to stop them. An Observer.

Mr. Harrison, who had no forces to stop an attack, did not even believe an attack possible, and merely sent on the letter to Joseph Flint, the agent general at Akassa. Flint received the letter at 7 A.M. on Monday, January 28, but was equally incredulous. He could not believe it possible that an attacking force could come from the direction of Brass without the vice-consul having definite knowledge of it.[8] Flint, however, "stationed himself on the night named at the head of the landing-stage, where he placed a quick-firing gun commanding the river, which is there three quarters of a mile wide." [9] There were seven steam launches available but Flint considered it necessary to get only one of them ready.

The attack was mounted exactly as the anonymous letter had predicted. The war canoes must have begun to gather at Nembe on Sunday, for on that day Father Bubendorfer saw "a large number of canoes covered with flags and armed with big guns five to six feet long. Usually one in the bows, one in the stern." It was on Monday at 9 A.M. that the Father saw King Koko again, back from the "palaver." The king was a changed man; "he had taken off a beautiful silk shirt, hat, etc., which he wore the day before, and he had only a cloth around his waist and his body was covered with chalk. Round his waist he had monkeys skulls hanging, round his ankles manillas [native money]." The king had to perform a ceremony. As he came out of his juju house, he sprinkled water on himself and everybody in his canoes did likewise. His principal wife came out and showered brown chalk on him, completing the action by throwing the remainder on the canoe as a blessing. While this was going on all the other canoes were massed outside and there was shooting of guns and shouting. The king finished his religious rites and started by 10 A.M., followed by the entire Nembe contingent.

The Father estimated that twenty war canoes and gigs left Nembe at 10 A.M. on Monday. The king's canoe alone carried sixty-three men. The total number of fighting men he estimates as "quite a thousand men." Reverend Ockiya gives the list of chiefs providing war canoes at Nembe as: from Ogbolomabiri, (1) King Frederick William Koko, (2) Chief Joseph Alagoa, (3) Edmund Natebo, (4) Daniel Opuene, (5) Thomas Ockiya, (9) Moses Ananagha, (10) Gam Dede, (11) Okoko, (12) Dogu, (13) Inengite, and (14) Ojoko; and from Bassambiri, (1) Chief Christopher Warri, (2) Felix Smoke Amabebe, (3) Youpele Ebifa, (4) Stephen Iboromo, (5) Kari, (6) Muna, (7) Egbelu, (8) David Kieriama, (9) Daniel Kalango, (10) Joseph Erenemienyo, and (11) Bokolo, whose canoe was captained by Samuel Olali. This list gives a total of twenty-five, differing from the Father's estimate by five.

The Father heard nothing about the contingents from Okpoma and Twon, which must have met the Nembe fleet at some prearranged estuary or bay of the Brass River. The following chiefs from Twon are reported to have supplied war canoes: (1) Chief William Sambo, (2) Uriah Cameroon, and (3) Shidi. From Okpoma came the canoes of (1) King Obu, (2) Chief Iti, captained by Aneri and (3) Digiboerigha. Okpoma and Twon accordingly supplied six canoes, making a grand total of thirty-one. Many other canoes ordinarily used for trade were also adapted for war — much as English sailors had to do in 1588 at the crisis of the Armada.

The fleet must have deliberately moved slowly and was probably also delayed by the need to join up with the contingents from Twon and Okpoma. Accordingly, leaving Nembe at 10 A.M. on Monday, January 28, they must have passed the Brass consulate that night, for they "slipped down the Brass River without the knowledge of the Consul, and favoured by the last of the ebb tide and darkness of the night (it being then new moon), as also by a heavy mist that hung over the river, they reached the open mouth near the sea unobserved by the guard boat, and crossing below the factory opened fire on the chief residence from a position where the shell gun placed at the pier head could not reach them." [10]

It was this fire the vice-consul heard from the consulate at Twon, Brass:

On the morning of the 29th at 4:30 A.M. heavy firing was heard in the direction of Akassa which is about twelve or fourteen miles from here . . . there was very little doubt Akassa had been attacked as all the chiefs and big men from Twon and Fish Twon were absent.[11]

At Akassa itself, Mr. Flint realized that all was lost as soon as his gun had been disabled, and he escaped in the steamboat with another European, giving up an Englishman, Captain Morgan, and two visiting naval officers for lost. These men were saved only by the timely appearance of the steamer "Bathurst." The war canoes withdrew into midstream, imagining it to be a naval vessel. The white men quickly escaped in this steamer. The krooboys and native employees of the Company in the machine shops and sheds situated about half a mile from the main settlement, however, were surprised and killed or captured. Twenty-four were reported killed in the fighting and their heads carried away as trophies. About seventy were made prisoners.

The attackers had their losses too. A total of four were killed. A son of Chief Dogu, Akemegha Dogu, was killed in Chief Felix Amabebe Smoke's canoe; Idoni in Daniel Kalango's; and two Okpoma men, Chief Igula and Debi.[12]

The Royal Niger Company also lost heavily in property. Akassa was the headquarters of the company on the lower Niger south of Asaba and its "most important depot," with "large stores of coal, produce awaiting shipment home, most expensive machinery, palm nut, machine shed, a commodious slip, printing office, treasury, . . . post office. . . ."[13] The treasury safe was opened and more than £2,000 in specie removed. "Trade goods, furniture, and fittings of all sorts were carried off, also breech-loading arms and ammunition. . . . But, in addition to what was stolen, still more injury was done by the destruction of the Company's books, records, and accounts, and by the skillful damage done to machinery by the removal of the more delicate parts where the machines themselves were too solid to be entirely ruined."[14] The masses of the fighting men were of course attracted by the vast quantities of gin discovered in the stores. It was all either drunk on the spot or carried home.

These doings must have taken some time to complete. The firing heard by Acting Vice-Consul Harrison at 4:30 A.M. continued until 6 A.M. of Tuesday, January 29. After that nothing happened until 5 P.M. of the same day, when Harrison saw "a shoal of apparently market canoes very much laded with produce" appear from the direction of Akassa. These were followed by "innumerable canoes, consisting of war canoes, gig canoes and small ones — as soon as they turned the corner of Akassa Creek each war canoe fired off its biggest gun.

The canoes kept passing until 7:15." [15] Harrison put the number of canoes at between forty and fifty, and the number of men in them at over 1,500.

Father Bubendorfer remained at Nembe after seeing the war canoes off on the morning of Monday, January 28. It was not until the following day, the day of the attack, that he learned the expedition had gone to Akassa, although the town had been denuded of all its male population. The king's brother and another chief (the Father called him Allan Moses) were left behind with the women, and the king instructed the Father to approach them if he needed anything. He observed that after the expedition left, custom prescribed that the women should not sleep inside their houses, but out in the yards.

The war canoes were again slow in making their way back to Nembe. Last seen from the consulate at 7:15 P.M. on Tuesday, the first war canoe arrived at Nembe at 9:45 A.M. on Wednesday, January 30, 1895. It was followed by all the others, and carried "the Company's big flag."

Wednesday was the day of sacrifice. The priests had a strong case. Ogidiga had given victory, and it was the custom on such occasions to carry out the *peripele* play at Sacrifice Island (Isikara), on which the prisoners were executed. There was also a smallpox epidemic, and the sacrifice of prisoners was thought necessary to stay it.

King Frederick William Koko led the way. His first port of call had in fact been Sacrifice Island and he did not come home until 2:30 P.M. "King Koko gave the orders for a general sacrifice of prisoners and canoes with much beating of drums and singing of songs went down towards Sacrifice Island — and returned — but now their occupants were all painted with white chalk — a sign that each man had killed at least one or two prisoners. . . ." [16]

However, there was a "Christian" party [17] of about eight chiefs and their followers who refused to take part in this business. Their leader, Chief Christopher Warri, himself had three prisoners — a Mrs. Price, an Assaye man and an Asaba boy. Chief Christopher Warri explained that a slaughter of prisoners was "against his principles," and also that these men would be useful to him later when he went up the Niger to trade. Many other chiefs expressed the idea that the killings were "against their feelings" and Chief Nathaniel Hardstone Yekorogha was so shocked "he could not bear to look on the slaughter and shut himself in his house." [18] It was mainly through the influence of these chiefs that many prisoners were later given up to the consul-general.

The booty collected at Akassa was not considered the property of individuals. It had to be pooled before division into individual lots. Two chiefs were chosen, Chief Okoko Oruwari of Ogbolomabiri and Chief Stephen Iboromo of Bassambiri, to invoke the gods to the effect that any person who held back the spoils of war from the common pool should die. The things were then divided into two parts — one for Ogbolomabiri and the other for Bassambiri. As there was no king, the Bassambiri chiefs subdivided their share equally among themselves. In Ogbolomabiri, the king took a third, and the chiefs took equal shares of the other two thirds.[19] Okpoma and Twon apparently took their own spoils away.

Both tradition and the official records agree that the raid on Akassa was the popular choice of the Nembe people after they had made up their mind that "To die by the sword was far better than to die of hunger." Sir Claude MacDonald, the commissioner and consul-general of the Niger Coast Protectorate, discovered that

Every single chief and headman in the Brass tribe took part in the attack, those only absent who were unable to attend through sickness; these were Chief Sambo of Twon and Chief Oboo of Fishtown whose war canoes were however present. Chief James Spiff and Kemmer were not present at the attack, as they were supposed to be too friendly with the Consulate and would probably give information; their retainers were there; their hearts undoubtedly so.[20]

It is known that the war canoes of Chief Sambo and of King Obu were present. The chief whose absence is most known is Chief James A. Spiff. He and his people of Gbobokiri were absent. It is strange for Sir Claude to think that it was possible for a chief to decide against a war and for his retainers to go. His war canoe and retainers might go without him, but only at his orders. The reason for James Spiff's decision not to go was obviously his friendship with the Niger Coast Protectorate government. He was known to be as hostile to the Royal Niger Company as anybody.[21] He had in fact presented the petition of 1889 to Sir Claude MacDonald.

Nembe had no allies at the attack, though the people of Akassa and other Ijaw villages in the neighbourhood rushed in after the attack to share in the plunder. Company officials later alleged that King Koko had intimidated and incited these peoples to join and that they had no grievances of their own against the company. At the Kirk Inquiry, the company admitted to having burnt down "Kiama, lower portion of Sabagreia, Tombia and Permoberi (Peremabiri)" for their participation. The only witness the company called to prove Nembe intimidation and incitement was Chief Nangi of Ekowe who said King Koko sent him a demijohn of rum and asked him to kill all company employees at Ekowe. But this was three days after the raid, and the rum was handed over to the company's station agent.

The consul-general himself observed that any Ijaw community that participated did so not because they were threatened with enslavement by Koko or because they were bribed. They had their own grievances against the company. They, as other primary producers, resented the restriction to a single buyer. Company retaliation and burning of hostile Ijaw towns and villages had been going on long before 1895.

Sir Claude also had information of Nembe emissaries to New Calabar (Kalabari) and Bonny. The letter to Bonny contained no threats. It enumerated Nembe grievances against the Royal Niger Company and called on the Bonny chiefs to help "as brethren." The Bonny chiefs gathered in plenary conferences to consider the appeal, but news arrived that the attack had already taken place. The letter was then handed over to the acting vice-consul, Mr. A. B. Harcourt.

THE BRITISH COUNTER ATTACK

Sir Claude MacDonald, commissioner and consul-general of the Niger Coast Protectorate, was cabled by Acting Vice-Consul Cuthbert E. Harrison and arrived at the Brass consulate from his headquarters in Calabar on February 2, 1895. Sir Claude immediately took the position that a state of war against Nembe existed and gave the chiefs till February 9 to surrender. He proceeded to put the consulate in a state of defense and began to concentrate forces from all parts of the Protectorate.

Sir Claude's argument would appear to be that the chiefs and people had committed an offence by taking the law into their own hands. It is true they had a strong case in their favor and it cannot be doubted that the removal of their ancient markets constituted great hardship for them. Nothing could be done about this, however, as the British government was itself responsible for granting the charter to the company and had apportioned the territory. By their action in taking the law into their own hands the people of Brass had embarrassed Her Majesty's government of the Niger Coast Protectorate. That government had been shown to have lacked the vigilance to prevent a native people from attacking "an adjoining friendly government." It could be interpreted as a sign of ineffective administration and of failure to fulfill Britain's civilizing mission. Moreover, charges of human sacrifice and cannibalism had been leveled — acts which offended against humanity and natural justice. If native tribes within the Protectorate were permitted to act in this way, the British flag and British prestige would be endangered in this part of the Empire.

The leaders of Nembe on their part tried to avoid death by the queen's sword. Soon after they returned from Akassa, a letter was dispatched to Acting Vice-Consul Harrison assuring him that they had no quarrel with the queen or her servants and that their quarrel was with the Royal Niger Company. This was on January 31, 1895. In reply to Sir Claude MacDonald's letter of February 3 giving an ultimatum for their surrender, the king and chiefs repeated the point that their rising was merely a protest against the oppression of the Royal Niger Company. This letter was dated February 4. On the same day the consul-general visited Twon. He met a chief who had not been at the attack on Akassa and was again assured that the people meant no harm to him or to any government official. The government had made up its mind to fight on behalf of the company, however, and the next few days were taken up with preparations for the counterattack.

On February 5, the consul-general received reinforcements of two officers and ninety-two men from Calabar. Mr. Flint and Captain Morgan of the company's constabulary also arrived. Captain Morgan showed several wounds he had received ten days earlier while burning an Ijaw town. Sir Claude also went to Akassa and ascertained that the company had a force of sixty Hausas and expected one hundred more from Lokoja.

Sir Claude tried to reconnoiter up the Nembe Creek on February 6. He received a warning the following day to give prior notice of his movements to avoid attack. The consul-general was surprised by the vigilance revealed by this letter: "We had seen nobody from the launch — but the bush had evidently been full of spies and very timely notice of our approach had been given." [22]

The consul-general again visited Akassa on February 9, to meet Admiral Bedford. The company had received its hundred auxilliaries from Lokoja, led by Captain Moloney. The captain, however, had been attacked on the Niger: "Captain Moloney had been very severely wounded . . . the disturbances were spreading up the Niger." [23]

The consul-general returned to Calabar for further reinforcements and stores. He came back on February 12:

> I returned to Brass and found the situation much the same, fighting was still going on in the River, the Brass District itself being quiet and the native chiefs both of Nembe and Fishtown sent me messages to say that their palaver was not with the Queen but with the Company and that so long as they were not allowed to go back to their old markets the war would not cease.[24]

February 15 was taken up with reconnoitering the approaches to Nembe and Okpoma (Fishtown). The consul-general himself, accompanied by Commander Marx, R.N., and Commander Grant-Dalton, came up to within six hundred yards of Okpoma. Captain Dundas and Lieutenant Child, both of the Protectorate marine department, charted a 14-foot channel "up to the mouth of the Nimbe Creek."

On February 14, the consul-general received telegraphic instructions from Lord Kimberley. He was to exact a moderate fine, confiscate guns and war canoes, and obtain the return of property plundered from the Royal Niger Company. He went to Akassa to see how much aid the company was ready to offer in the attack on Nembe. The company offered only a ship and no troops. Before he returned to the consulate with Admiral Bedford, the consul watched the company's troops attack a stockaded town. It was a combined operation. The stockades were first destroyed by shell from H.M.S. "Thrush." The company's troops then advanced and took the town without resistance. The town, which was opposite the company's settlement, was full of plunder.

More reinforcements arrived on the eighteenth. Captain H. L.

Gallwey and Major Leonard also arrived from the Benin and Warri districts. The consul wrote to the chiefs to give up their war canoes and what they had carried away from Akassa.

On the following day, February 19, a plan of attack was made. It was decided to send a main party against Nembe and a smaller one against towns on the Ekole Creek (Onitoru). This plan was scrapped after a reply was received from King Koko asking for a "little time to think," and after it was learned that vigorous stockade operations were going on at Nembe. A new plan was evolved, combining everything and everyone for a massive attack on Nembe. The entire force started from the consulate at 11 A.M.

The Protectorate force, together with two steamers lent by the Niger Company (Yakoba and Nupe), entered the Nembe Creek at 2 P.M. and arrived in front of Sacrifice Isand by 4:30 P.M. Their passage was blocked by "a very skillfully constructed obstruction stretching right across the creek."

This obstruction consisted of a treble tier of heavy timbers driven into the mud with cross timbers, the whole clamped together with iron. This obstruction must have taken 500 men a week to make consisting as it did of upwards of 2,000 heavy bolts of timber.

With the use of gun cotton a passage was soon blown through the obstruction and the force proceeded to land on Sacrifice Island (Isikara), which they wanted to use as a base.

It can hardly be imagined that all this activity had been unobserved. It is told [25] how spies had been stationed at Kalabilema Creek some miles to the mouth of Nembe Creek. The agreed signal — a cannon shot — was given when the protectorate force was observed at this point. The people of Nembe accordingly knew of the approach of the enemy before the protectorate force entered the Nembe Creek at 2 P.M. and by the time the force arrived off Sacrifice Island the war canoes had taken positions of vantage for an attack.

The news that the enemy was coming was received with tumult and confused shouting and singing of war songs. Men and women rushed in a body towards Tombi — the part of the town where the enemy would normally make his first appearance. The excitement was caused by the realization that a crisis in the history of the city-state had arrived. In all the city-state's history no enemy had brought war to the metropolis. It was considered impregnable and the belief

was that Ogidiga would not allow an enemy force to appear before
Nembe. It was customary for the war canoes of Nembe to go out
to meet the enemy in his own waters, at his own gates. The unheard
of was coming to pass! When the crowd reached Tombi, King Koko
called a halt and ordered the war canoes to be immediately readied
to go out to meet the foe.

The war canoes must have been watching Sir Claude MacDonald
and his men as they blew up the obstruction and began to clear
Sacrifice Island to establish a base. He describes what followed:

Hardly had the work been commenced when from the various creeks
which lead into the lagoon . . . facing the island came a large number
of war canoes generally estimated at about 20 each manned by about 60
paddlers and armed men and advanced with colours flying and tom toms
beating — they came on in a menacing manner and Lieutenant Taylor
R.N. since killed deemed it advisable to fire a shot from his 3 pounder
in front of the leading canoe. No sooner had the smoke cleared away
when a heavy rifle and cannon fire was opened from the canoes, the
cannon balls and bullets came crashing and whistling through the trees
and brushwood on the island but without causing any casualties on our
side, fire was immediately opened on the canoes and a brisk little fight
ensued resulting in the sinking of three canoes. . . . The rest of the
canoes then made off. These canoes were all flying flags with the names
of their owners, prominent amongst them being King Koko and Chief
Allogoa [Chief Joseph Alagoa].

The consul-general's account agrees in essentials with oral tradition. It is of course assumed that there were losses on the protectorate
side, but both sinking of war canoes and the final retreat are admitted.
Two war canoes are specifically mentioned for the heavy losses they
suffered. In Chief Gam Dede's war canoe all but the chief and four
others were wounded. A ball struck a post in Chief Okoko Oruwari's
canoe and the canoe sank. Two, including the gunner at the bow,
were killed. Other war canoes had losses.

On the morning of the twentieth the consul-general and Admiral
Bedford sent an ultimatum from Sacrifice Island (two miles from
the town). They pointed out that the chiefs had fired on the queen's
forces and must surrender as previously ordered. An answer was
returned by 5 P.M. with the flag of truce that had carried the ultimatum:

. . . the chiefs in their answer to me said that they were sorry for having fired on the Queen's troops but mistook the white ensign for the white flag of the Company — They added that they would give up their war canoes and loot if they had more time and if the Admiral would remove all his ships and launches.

It was decided not to return an answer to this diplomatic note but to proceed with preparations for an attack on the town. Buoys had to be planted across the lagoon and a safe channel explored to Tombi — the quarter of Chief Joseph Alagoa. At the point where the creek opened on Tombi an uncompleted stockade was found pierced for six guns. This too was destroyed with gun cotton by Lieutenant Calthorpe.

The attack was mounted on the morning of February 22, 1895, on the orders of Admiral Bedford. The creek leading to Tombi (Tamama) was entered at 5:45 A.M. and by 6:15 A.M. the forces "were heavily engaged at Allogoa's and another in the Town which opened a very effective fire on the right flank of the attack. It was here that most of the casualties occurred." The casualties of the protectorate force at Tombi included Lieutenant Taylor and two bluejackets shot dead, a bluejacket and four others wounded. The defenders of Chief Alagoa's house were finally driven out leaving behind four or five dead "including Chief Allogoa's nephew who was found dead by the side of the gun he had just fired."

The attacking force disembarked at Tombi and proceeded to skirmish through the town. The next position they stormed and took was Chief Opuene's house. Fire was opened on them here from a position on the opposite bank of the creek:

. . . upon this [Chief Opuene's house] a very brisk fire was opened. The batteries of Chief Warri, Kari and Kalango on the creek where the boats of the navy were expected to appear did not do any damage [had the boats come round the corner of the mission point they would have been roughly handled].

The riflemen in the above mentioned batteries soon found the range and a fairly smart rifle fire was opened on Chief Opuene's house the shot striking the iron roof of his house and also the church and mission. . . .

This position was never taken as it was "seen to be heavily stockaded and defended."

It was 10:30 A.M. before a further advance took Chief Nathaniel

Hardstone Yekorogha's house. As the protectorate forces entered this house, defense batteries from chiefs Kalango's and Egbelu's houses opened fire on it —"most of the shot from their guns were passing overhead though one or two fell in the adjacent mud and one went right through Yekoroga's house. . . ." The forces later skirmished through the rest of Ogbolomabiri, putting houses on fire. They then retired to rest and consult in Chief Opuene's house, intending to attack Bassambiri in the afternoon. It was decided to leave, and the retreat was begun at 3 P.M.; by sunset of the twenty-second the punitive force of the Niger Coast Protectorate government had withdrawn from Nembe to the Brass River and was on its way to the consulate.

Sir Claude MacDonald was satisfied that Nembe had received sufficient punishment, but he was also impressed with the courage shown by the people in its defense. He summarized the result of the counterattack on the metropolis as follows:

In Nembe the King's house, and the houses belonging to Chiefs had been totally demolished with gun cotton and the native houses burnt. The houses and huts of the poor people in Bassambiri had fared better but the Chief's European houses notably that of Chief Christopher Warri were riddled with projectiles from 3 pounder quick firing guns, 7 pounder mountain guns, and 9 and 24 pounder war rockets.[26]

Sir Claude's estimate of losses on the Nembe side was three hundred or more because

7,872 Martin Henry rounds had been fired at them at ranges varying from 400 to 800 yards as well as 63 rounds of shrapnel shell by the Protectorate troops alone, and more than double that number by the other forces engaged. . . .[29]

Sir Claude remarks that the defenders took very good cover and fought from well-stockaded positions; he would have put the estimate of losses even higher but for this fact. But local accounts of the number killed in the actual fighting is many times smaller than the consul-general's "conservative" estimate. A total of five men are said to have been killed at Tombi, including Posi, the gallant defender Sir Claude describes as Chief Alagoa's nephew and the man who was found dead "by the side of the gun he had just fired." Sir Claude himself observed only about five bodies at Tombi but his explanation was that many more had been carried away by the Nembemen, who actually did remove bodies for fear of the enemy mutilating their comrades' corpses. A woman is also reported to have been hit at Amasarapolo and Chief Abedi at Bassambiri. This makes a total of seven killed during the fighting at Nembe. A loss of some further seven is recorded for the engagement off Sacrifice Island in the lagoon.

The losses on the side of the attackers was given by Sir Claude MacDonald as Lieutenant Taylor and two bluejackets killed, one bluejacket with a leg shot off, and four others wounded. All this was at Tombi. No other casualties were reported.

After Nembe had been taken, no further difficulty was experienced in burning Okpoma and Twon. An ultimatum was sent to both towns on February 24. On the twenty-fifth H.M.S. "Barrosa" and H.M.S. "Widgeon" went up to within 2,000 to 4,000 yards of Okpoma and shelled it. This shelling provided a cover for a force of one-hundred-and-fifty protectorate infantry and fifty Niger Company constabulary to march through the bush under the command of Captain Gallwey to take the town in the rear. The town had been deserted and "two formidable stockade batteries" in the place blown up with gun cotton. The town was burned to the ground.

On the twenty-sixth the troops occupied Twon but here "the houses and plantations of the poor people were left standing." Only two houses, both "two-storied European built structures," were burned. The Consul General states as his reason for this special treatment given to Twon the fact that "though the people took part in the attack on Akassa, they held aloof when the atrocities were committed." [28]

There is no evidence given that Okpoma (Fishtown) did take part in the "atrocities." Two possibilities may be suggested to explain why the forces found it simpler to destroy all houses at Okpoma. It may have been difficult to distinguish the houses of chiefs from those of the poor people. There seems to have been a ruling of the town's deity that no European-type structures be erected in Okpoma. Also, the chiefs may not have been as rich as those of Nembe and Twon, as the Okpoma chiefs do not appear to have been as active in the European trade as the others. In any case the Protectorate government had no love for Okpoma. Two years before (1893) the people of Okpoma had threatened to destroy the consulate and the merchants' factories at Twon, Brass. Two hundred protectorate troops had to be concentrated in a hurry. Kirk reports that Okpoma was then regarded as "a nest of pirates — the same people who took so prominent a part in the attack on Akassa that it was thought necessary this year to destroy their town." [29] The total destruction of Okpoma thus came about partly because of the prominent part it played at Akassa.

WAR DAMAGES

By February 26, 1895, the British counteroffensive was completed. It was then time to devote attention to exacting war damages from the people, and to carry out Lord Kimberley's instruction of the sixteenth to (1) exact a fine, (2) confiscate guns and war canoes, and (3) effect a return of plunder.

The consul-general started on this stage of his duties by writing to the chiefs informing them that he was satisfied with the punishment meted out to them and that he was prepared to accept their surrender. He made an exception, however, in the case of King Koko: ". . . for whose capture alive I offered a reward of £200. This chief I have ascertained has been the leading spirit in this movement. He has been in the receipt of a subsidy of £200 a year from the protectorate Government which he has spent upon himself and not in opening new markets for the good of his people." [30]

The consul received the cooperation of the chiefs and even of the king in his efforts to obtain reparation. But there was no surrender or betrayal of persons. The statement about £200 subsidy is obviously an error since Koko was paid no more than £30 a year from 1891. In any case, after the Niger Company had settled down at Akassa there was little scope for King Koko to open new markets. The "movement" he was leading was in itself in the interests of his people — an attempt to reopen old markets.

A total fine of £516 was assessed by the consul-general as compensation for the prisoners killed at Nembe. By the first of May, half of this sum had been paid by the chiefs in the form of checks drawn on the British merchants on the river.

War canoes were voluntarily given up by the chiefs. Eighteen were tied up "to the mangrove bush at the end of the Nimbe Creek, fourteen miles from the Settlement," [31] and were towed by the yacht "Evangeline." A total of twenty-three canoes used at the attack were surrendered. Guns and ammunition taken from Akassa was returned over a long period, and some heavy guns owned by chiefs were spiked.

The restoration of plunder was not very successful, since much of it consisted of perishable goods. The gin had been drunk and the specie "scattered or melted down." But Sir Claude collected five hundred Maria Theresa thalers, "12 boats and canoes taken at Akassa, as well as the Maxim gun and Brase Romitzer, with ammunition for the former."

With the help of chiefs James Spiff and Christopher Warri, and the cooperation of King Frederick William Koko, twenty-five prisoners were returned. And after Sir John Kirk had raised the point in June at the Inquiry, the skulls of the Company employees killed in the war at Akassa and Sacrifice Island were returned in July.

In a dispatch of May 1, Sir Claude MacDonald summarized the punitive measures he had taken against the people. Nembe, Twon, Okpoma (Big Fishtown) and Ewoama (Little Fishtown) had been burned, and the people had fled into the bush or to remote villages. In Sir Claude's own words:

The following sums up the punishment meted out to the Brass men for their attack on Akassa and subsequent atrocities at Nimbe. They had been in a state of siege for over two months, they had given up all war canoes and their cannon, and as much loot as remained, their towns had been demolished, and more particularly by the destruction of Nimbe, which town they had looked upon as impregnable, their pride most grievously humbled, those chiefs who had been guilty of cannibalistic sacrifices had been fined, the fine in aggregate amounting to £516: =: = d and numbers of their people were starving in the jungle and dying of small pox.[32]

Oral tradition confirms the claim that the people of Okpoma and Twon fled into the bush, and many chiefs and people at Nembe removed to villages in the interior. The smallpox, for which the priests had demanded the sacrifices, had apparently not subsided, and it claimed more lives than the hostilities. The killing of prisoners was, however, strictly for ritual purposes, and it was not true that a few chiefs alone would bear the burden of the fines imposed. The payment of the fines was the collective responsibility of the city-state. Sir Claude also observed that in this confusion livestock was indiscriminately destroyed, and there was loss or destruction of other sources of food. As long as the protectorate troops were around Twon and the naval vessels were on the river, and as long as the consul-general had not made formal peace, the people could not go to their markets freely to buy food. It was the suffering occasioned by the smallpox and the shortage of food supplies that induced Archdeacon Crowther and the missionaries at Bonny as well as Proctor, the European missionary at Twon, to appeal to the consul-general to make a speedy settlement.

THE KIRK INQUIRY

Lord Kimberley was completely convinced by the consul-general's dispatch and decided to seek a settlement. He also listened to the agitation in Parliament and outside, from those who were opposed to the company's monopoly. Their sympathy with the Nembe attack led to an investigation into the administration of the company. Sir John Kirk was chosen as commissioner. He had been British consul-general at Zanzibar, a director of the Imperial British East Africa Company, and was a British representative at the Brussels Conference.

Kirk arrived in Nigeria on June 6 and left by the end of the month. He agreed that the Niger Company had been monopolistic and that its regulations kept the Nembe traders from their traditional markets, but he argued that it was the British government which was to blame for granting the charter and for approving the company's regulations. Moreover, the company was trying to carry out the provisions of the Brussels Acts against the importation of arms and ammunition. The whole affair was shown to be a result of circumstances, and nobody was to blame except, perhaps, the British government.

Kirk was clearly convinced that the company's regulations kept traders from the Niger. Any trader was "required to pay a sum of 50 pounds for license to trade, with a further sum of ten pounds, also yearly, for every station he traded at, and he would then be allowed to trade at such stations as had been declared open for that purpose, and no where else. He would next be required to pay 100 pounds annually if he intended to trade in spirits, without which . . . trade in the Delta is at present impossible." After paying these fees and licenses, the trader had still to report at Akassa and pay a duty of two shillings per gallon on his trade spirits, after having already paid one shilling a gallon at Brass. On completing business, he would again report, and pay an export duty of 20 per cent on the value of all produce.

The remedy suggested was for the government to allow free trade in the coastal Niger territory.[33] The idea was to continue the company in administrative control of the area, but to form a customs union with the Niger Coast Protectorate government. The company was then to pay interest to its shareholders from the administration of customs.

THE FINAL SETTLEMENT

Kirk's recommendations would have pleased Lord Kimberley and the Liberal government, but in June 1895 Lord Salisbury's Conservative government had taken over, and Chamberlain had to deal with this matter. Chamberlain's ideas of expanding and developing the "estate" of the empire were not compatible with the continuance of company rule. Kirk's recommendations were clearly unacceptable to Chamberlain, and no final arrangement could be arrived at until 1899. The government of the Niger Coast Protectorate and the Royal Niger Company had on their part to agree on interim measures in order to prevent a recurrence of the January incident.

In the local negotiations that followed, King Koko declined on all occasions to meet the consul-general and the representatives of the company. Sir Ralph Moore, the new consul-general, concluded from this that

There is no doubt that he is entirely antagonistic to the Government and the course he pursues, in declining when possible all intercourse with the whiteman, is with a view to retaining his power, as "Juju Man," over the natives and posing as the absolute ruler of the country.[34]

The consul-general also complained that the Amassoma area opened to the Nembe people after Kirk's inquiry had again been closed by the company, and that only the Ekole Creek (Onitoru) was left open.

On April 1, 1896, Sir Ralph Moore issued a proclamation at Nembe containing the terms of "a temporary arrangement" that had been made for the benefit of the people. By this arrangement "the Ekole Creek and all creeks south of the Ekole Creek connecting with the River Niger will be opened to within one mile of the Niger for Brassmen to trade but the representative Chiefs will require to signify the adhesion of the Brass traders to this arrangement which is however of only a temporary nature pending the final settlement of the entire question of the markets." [35]

King Koko had again refused to attend the meeting preceding

the presentation of the proclamation, and it was explained that the terms of the arrangement might have been better if the king had been more friendly.

The reference to "the representative Chiefs" indicates the decision of the Protectorate government to set up a "native council" to take the place of King Koko in local government. This was done before the end of 1896. The council was comprised of Chiefs Nathaniel Hardstone Yekorogha, Thomas Ockiya, and Edmund Natebo of Ogbolomabiri; Christopher Warri, Felix Smoke Amabebe, and Daniel Kalango of Bassambiri; Chiefs Cameron, Spiff, N. Shidi, and I. Sambo of Twon; Atari, Eleke, and Necke of Okpoma.

The final settlement promised in the proclamation did not come until the end of 1899, when new arrangements were made for the administration of the whole of Nigeria. The charter of the Royal Niger Company was revoked and it became the Niger Company, a purely commercial firm with no administrative rights and no monopoly. The territory it administered in the lower Niger was merged with the Niger Coast Protectorate, which then became the Protectorate of Southern Nigeria. The company's sphere to the north was made the Protectorate of Northern Nigeria. The Colony and Protectorate of Lagos formed the third administrative unit in Nigeria.

The Niger Company was compensated by payments totaling 565,000 pounds, plus the right to certain mining royalties. The payments were broken down into 150,000 pounds "for the interruption and dislocation of business," 300,000 pounds for sums advanced by the company for purposes of administration, and 115,000 pounds for stores and property taken over from the company. The government was also to pay half of all royalties for ninety-nine years to the company for minerals in Northern Nigeria from an area "bounded on the West by the main stream of the Niger and on the East by a line running direct from Yola towards Zinder. . . ."[36]

Among the factors that led to the abrogation of the Royal Niger Company's charter, the Akassa war and the attendant publicity was one of the most important, though it was not, perhaps, a decisive factor. The British government was committed to a forward imperial policy, and in the high noon of imperial scramble in Africa, it was no longer safe to allow a private company to represent the state. The West African Frontier Force had been organized by Lugard and it was necessary for the government to send its own functionaries to consolidate the frontiers made with the French and Germans in Northern Nigeria. In this context the added appeal of serving the interests of indigenous peoples — as was provided by the case of Nembe — was not to be lightly dismissed.

By the time the settlement was made, however, the economic consequences of the new system imposed by the company's monopoly had already set. Trade had been permanently diverted to other rivers than the Brass; the Forcados and other Delta estuaries used by the company in reaching the Niger had become the main centers. The middleman had also become a thing of the past. In other ways, too, the incidents of 1895 marked a dividing point. After 1895 the traditional order began to crumble very fast, and with the retirement of King Koko the forces of change took control.

8

THE PRICE OF PROGRESS

In August 1920, thirty chiefs of Nembe presented a petition to the governor of Nigeria. It asked for a variety of modern amenities, among others that the area be included in the circuit of the supreme court sessions; that the doctor formerly stationed at Brass and removed during the war be returned and that a hospital be established; that a full and adequate post office be set up at the consulate, Twon, and a postal agency at Nembe; that, as currency notes were refused by the up-country farmers, coins be supplied in sufficient quantity; that tax on canoes be discontinued; and that steps be taken to revive the trade of Brass as a port.

Finally, the chiefs submitted a memorandum on House Rule, calling on the government to set aside the House Rule Ordinance, and restore the ancient system in its pure form. Captain Wauton's comments on the last demand was that the chiefs "naturally resent the abolition of the House Rule, and the loosening of their control over the people. I have repeatedly pointed out to them that this is the inevitable result of civilization." [1]

The dislocation of the House Rule system was only one instance of indigenous institutions disorganized by the influences attendant on the introduction of *Pax Britannica*. The chiefs evidently considered it too great a price to pay for progress. They would accept the material benefits of Western civilization but rejected its ideas of government and the corroding influence of the growing individualism fostered by these ideas and by the new social and economic order.

117

The influence of European ideas started to penetrate after 1895, when direct government authority began to be established. The supercargo of pregovernment days was a bird of passage and was often not himself equipped to carry the light of civilization. Men like Lake, Captain of the "Thomas of Liverpool," were rightly termed the palm oil ruffians. Captain Lake's action in snatching the Lander brothers from King Boy without paying the ransom agreed upon was not calculated to create respect for him or for his race. These traders, especially during the slave trade, brought very little more than guns and liquor; these articles in their turn bred violence and drunkenness. Their contact with the people was very brief and they perhaps had little opportunity to show anything but the baser parts of their nature.

After the palm oil trade had finally driven out slave traffic, the position began to improve. Friendship began to develop between white and black traders. Some trading chiefs even began to give theirs sons or close relations to serve with their friends to learn the white man's ways. The courts of equity became the forum of discussion of trade relations and the settlement of disputes. Chiefs and supercargoes had dinner parties together. It was in these times that the chiefs and princes on the Oil Rivers began to learn the power of Britain through her gun boats and through the British consul, but the effective direction of affairs still lay with the people.

Sir Claude MacDonald installed vice-consuls in all the rivers after 1891. This meant that the chiefs of these rivers no longer collected their customary dues. They now received them through the British authority. But even at this time the vice-consuls do not appear to have taken any interest in the internal affairs of the city-states. Sir John Kirk remarked of Vice-Consul Harper Moore at Brass that he "was not in touch with the population, and probably knew nothing of what went on outside the walls of his house." [2] This may have been an exaggeration, but it was based on facts. Mr. Harrison, who took over from Moore, was in no closer contact with the people when the 1895 Akassa raid happened.

British rule began to have a direct effect on the lives of the people when, in 1896, King Frederick William Koko was driven to self-exile and a native council was established. In the council the consuls had an instrument for carrying out the will of the government of the Niger Coast Protectorate. The members of the council had been selected for their cooperation with the government. This way to favor was of course easily learned, and the more the chiefs came to rely on the support of the British officers the more they lost influence with the people. The people also learned that they could equally look to the British authority for the reddress of wrongs and could even damage the record of a chief by allegations. A House member refusing to pay his tax to his House head could claim that the chief was reviving "indigenous forms of slave-owning."

When the chiefs protested against the withdrawal of the House Rule Ordinance, it was easy to see that they were fighting against "the loosening of their control over the people." The fact was that the loosening of control permitted the energetic members of the House to fend for themselves and strike out in new directions. The chief could no longer utilize the manpower of his House to make himself a big and successful trader, but the masses of his people, who were neither dynamic, progressive, nor self-sufficient, still looked to the chief to carry out his ancient customary duties.

Sir Ralph Moore's native councils of 1896 were constituted into native courts by Proclamation No. 25 of 1901. Two courts were thus recognized—the Nembe court (comprising the councilors from Ogbolomabiri and Bassambiri) and the Twon native court (comprising the chiefs of Twon and Okpoma). By the provisions of the Native Authority Ordinance published in 1916, the Twon native court and Chief Joseph Alagoa were appointed native authorities. But at a later date individual chiefs were appointed native authority for single native court areas as follows:

Chief Uriah Cameron—native authority for Twon, Brass native court area;

Chief Joseph Alagoa—native authority for Nembe native court area;
Chief Nangi (or Mangi) or Ekowe—native authority for Ijaw district of Brass division.

These native authorities were to be the local representatives of government. They did not carry out any direct administrative duties, but they generally watched the interests of government and saw that peace and order were maintained. There were no amanyanabo at Nembe from the time of the death of King Koko in 1898 until the reigns of Albert Oguara in 1924 at Bassambiri and the Reverend Anthony Ockiya in 1926 at Ogbolomabiri. The government accordingly appointed these native authorities as the single persons to be held directly responsible for the good conduct of their people. The native courts continued to serve as the main judicial authority, side by side with the native authority.

The memory of Chief Joseph Alagoa as native authority in Nembe during the long period of interregnum has remained fresh. He had fought against the white man in 1895 but had become convinced that further resistance was of no avail. At the turn of the century he alone remained of the old chiefs of the last half of the nineteenth century. He was an old man respected by all as a peace-loving and fair-minded authority on all questions of native custom and usage. His authority was rarely challenged and, as new territory was added to the Nembe court area, his influence and that of Nembe spread to such outlying districts as Emelego and Saka. Until his death on July 28, 1934, at the age of from one-hundred to one-hundred-and-twenty years, not even Kings Ognara and Anthony Ockiya had found cause to question his authority.

A further change in the system of local authority came after 1928. In that year direct taxation was started and in the following year a native administration was established with a native treasury. This reinforced the growing tendency for all authorities, including the amanyanabo, to become merely local functionaries of the colonial government. There is no doubt that the first amanyanabo under the new order — the Reverend Anthony Ockiya — suffered at the hands of his people for his dependence on government support. Some five years after his coronation, a faction decided that he was too subservient to government and declared him deposed. When the administrative officer called to settle the problem, the chiefs testily declared that they were the owners of the town and that they did not take kindly to interference:

No stranger should come to arrange our town for us. We want the Government to consult us if they want to do something in the town. . . .[3]

Chiefs at Nembe resented the intervention of the district officer on two grounds. First, some old chiefs considered it a shame that white officers who were invariably younger men should come to teach them how to rule. Second, the chiefs resented the paternal attitude adopted by some officers. Even when this attitude was not shown in behavior, it was implied by the fact that these officers had to review cases previously settled by the chiefs. In view of the fact

that such settlements were made according to "native law and custom," they could not understand how young British officers could
be more knowledgeable.

It may not be inferred from this that the benefits of *Pax Britannica* were not appreciated by the chiefs and people. They were impressed by Western technology, and the peace that now prevails
between peoples is a source of enduring astonishment to the old
people. For example, they never fail to express this astonishment
whenever one of their children returns safely from a long trip.

THE CHRISTIAN MISSION

The word of God was first preached in the Brass district by Captain Pearman, an agent of Hatton Cookson and Company.[4] A weekly
service was held on board the Captain's hulk on the Brass River.
Early in 1861, a missionary, the Reverend J. G. Taylor, was established at Akassa, and he paid visits to the congregation at Brass.

In 1862 Bishop Crowther visited King Kien at his residence in
Tombi, Nembe. The king refused to permit any missionary work
among his people.

Kien's successor, King Ockiya (1863–79), was to be the friend of
the missionaries. In 1867 he met the Archdeacon D. C. Crowther
in the Akassa Creek and called to him: "God-man, God-man, come
near. I wish to speak to you; I have been asking for you." The king
asked that Christianity be planted in Nembe as had been done at
Bonny. Accordingly, on August 25, 1868, a school-chapel was established at Twon, the people footing half the bill. Bishop Crowther
visited Nembe again in October 1869, and both King Ockiya and
Arisimo agreed to let the new religion grow without interference.
Even Bokolo, the high priest of the national god, agreed to the
establishment of the new mission. The bishop was charmed with
everybody:

King Ockiya is a tall, stout, well-built man, of a calm, kind, and unassum-
ing appearance, withal sensible and honest. Bokolo the priest is really a
fine-looking man.

In spite of the early promise the mission was confined to Twon
and church members at Nembe had to travel some thirty miles to
attend service. And when the Reverend Thomas Johnson visited
Nembe in January 1870, he found King Arisimo not so willing to

see the new religion come to Bassambiri. Another Bassambiri chief, Isemia (Isemiyai Pegi), engaged in an argument with the pastor. The chief declared that his offerings of fowls and goats to his gods had saved his son from death. The pastor affirmed there were no gods but God. The chief pointed out that God created the lesser gods to look after man. The pastor said these gods were the invention of man. The Chief's answer was "Never mind; let us drop the conversation for a better time."

The arguments about the place of the new religion in Nembe society became urgent after a church was established in the metropolis. King Ockiya started keeping prayer meetings at home in 1872. In 1877 he called for donations and soon a church was erected at Ewoama. And in 1881 the Reverend J. D. Garrick was ordained and sent to Nembe.

The decade after 1880 would appear to have been the vintage years for the church. Sir Claud MacDonald observed in 1895:

In 1889 when I visited this river, I attended Divine Service . . . a congregation of some 900 men, women and children followed the service with much apparent attention. There is a large iron Church and Schools at Twon, also at Nimbe, but the once large congregations have dwindled down to almost a handful.[5]

Sir Claude observed that in 1895 the churches were not only empty but also in disrepair. A clergyman with whom he discussed the matter explained that poor attendance was due to bad trade on the Brass River.

Sir Claude MacDonald, attempting to make out the case of the chiefs at the Kirk Inquiry on the subject of human sacrifice, and the influence of the so-called Christian party, discovered that:

Some years ago the Christian party was much stronger and more powerful than their opponents, many chiefs who were brought up as Christians have now gone back to fetishism, amongst these King Koko, the reason for this being that they had lost faith in the white man's God, who had allowed them to be oppressed, and their trade, their only means of livelihood, to be taken from them without just cause or reason.[6]

Sir John Kirk's own finding was that neither the missionaries nor the government officials had understood the people. They had not learned the local tongue and could not therefore communicate properly with them. According to Kirk, Christian teaching had never yet gone beyond the surface. C. N. de Cardi,[7] an observant British merchant on the Brass River, also concluded that the missionaries had largely failed. His theory was that the Christian faith was completely opposed to the institutions of the people. He singled out polygyny and "domestic slavery" (the House system) as being specially responsible for the people's refusal to accept Christianity.

There is in fact little doubt that the missionaries presented Christianity as the direct antithesis of everything the people believed in. We are told that the missionaries in biblical times, when they saw a statue to an unknown god, tried to identify their own God with the people's unknown god. The Rev. T. Johnson's argument with Chief Isemia in 1870 shows that the missionaries of the last century tried rather to discredit all of the peoples' beliefs and customs. They tried to sweep everything away — tried to work on a completely clean slate. A people had pride in what their fathers and grandfathers had handed down and could not but feel offended at this attitude.

A result of this approach was that Christianity was looked upon as a foreign innovation, in the same sense that the government and the Royal Niger Company were foreign intruders. The God of the missionaries was indeed "the white man's God" and was responsible for the changes and misfortunes attendant on the intrusion of white economic imperialism. It is instructive to note that every outbreak of smallpox after 1868 was seen to be a result of Christian activity or the result of the anger of the gods at the establishment of Christianity. Riots and persecution followed.

These outbreaks, in their turn, divided the community into two — the "heathens" and the self-righteous "Christian," the former sullen and the latter aggressive and triumphantly identifying themselves with the prestige of the white man's civilization. When King Ockiya, Mingi VII, died in 1879, the Christians tried to seize the body to perform their own rites of burial. The King's brother, Chief Berena, stood for the customary procedure, and a civil war ensued. Chief Berena and his party seized two members of the Christian party — Thomas D. Ockiya and Moses Ananagha Ockiya. The Christians also captured Izulu — a nephew of both Berena and the late king. This was indeed a case of brother rising against brother and son against father. In the end it was decided that each party should perform its own rites. And this has become the rule even at the coronation, where the traditional ceremony is followed by a Christian service.

The result of this situation is a dualism in the character of the younger generation. In the mission schools they had been taught to regard the customs of their fathers as vaguely degrading. Many of these customs have accordingly been allowed to die gradually. At the same time they are haunted by the ancient beliefs of their people and cannot grasp Christian teaching in its entirety.

Like other Nigerians and peoples everywhere who have had to take in new ideas and encounter new forces, the people of Nembe have found progress a difficult thing.

REFERENCE MATTER

APPENDIX I

KING LISTS: NEMBE, OKPOMA, ODIOMA

Tepowa's List (1907)

1. Ekule 2. Ogbodo 3. Nembe 4. Owagi 5. Peresuo 6. Obia

Ogbolomabiri		Bassambiri	
1. Mingi	6. Amain	1. Ogbodo	6. Mein
2. Ikata	7. Kien	2. Okiriai	7. Dugurai
3. Gboro	8. Ockiya	3. Gbolowe	8. Arishima
4. Kuki	9. Koko	4. Tamono	9. Ebifa
5. Kulo		5. Kariai	

Dickinson's List (1932)

1. Ogbolo	6. Owagi	11. Peresuo
2. Kala-Ekule	7. Kala-Igula	12. Ekutia (regent)
3. Nembe	8. Ogbolo	13. Obia (regent)
4. Opu-Igula	9. Opu-Basuo	14. Kala-Basuo
5. Amein	10. Ogio	

Ogbolomabiri		Bassambiri
1. Mingi	6. Kien	1. Ogbodo
2. Gboro	7. Ockiya	2. Gbolowei
3. Ikata	8. Koko	3. Warri
4. Kulo	9. Rev. A. Ockiya	4. Dede
5. Amain		5. Tamono
		6. Kariyai
		7. Mein
		8. Duguruyai
		9. Arisima
		10. Ebifa
		11. Albert Igeora [Oguara]
		12. Ben Warri

Sources: A. Tepowa, "A Short History of Brass and Its People," *Journal of the African Society*, 1907; E. N. Dickinson, Assistant District Officer, "An Intelligence Report on the Nembe Clan," 1932.

Note: The list at Chapter 4 follows Tepowa with a few changes. Ogio has been added between Owagi and Peresuo. In the Ogbolomabiri list, Kuki has been removed, and the two kings after Koko (Anthony Ockiya, and Francis Allagoa) added. In the Bassambiri list, Okiriai has been deleted, and the two kings after Ebifa (Albert Oguara and Ben Warri) added. The accepted modern spelling of names has been followed in Chapter 4.

LIST OF KINGS OF OKPOMA

Okpo
Sikaka
Ibelubelu
Nede
Tia
Kpekiya
Saikiri
Osungu
Onu
Akirigbo
Gboro
Boyo
Orukare
Goli
Obasi
Obu
Okiringbo
Robert Okparan Tubu
R. M. Elei Tamonobere 1957–

Note: The following served as regents: (1) Burufegha after Goli; (2) Isele after Sagbe Obasi; (3) Eleke after Obu; (4) Jacob Obasi after Okiringbo. The list was obtained from Mr. J. S. Berena, Town Clerk Okpoma.

LIST OF KINGS OF ODIOMA

Igoni
Kala-Igoni
Okolo
Pegi
Ikagi
Duguruyai
Eminigi
Itabala

Orukari
Agbala
Tubo
Dounya
Polo
Okolo
Olunta

Note: Mr. S. G. Kpokiri, who supplied the list, adds that Odioma is the only survivor of fourteen original settlements at the St. Nicholas estuary. Each of these towns had its own line of kings, and the remains of some of them can still be traced at the sites. The name Odioma was itself derived from Odio, the wife of the founder, Igoni. She became a famous herbalist and the crowds who flocked to her always said they were going to Odio's town, that is, Odio-ama.

The names of the fourteen original villages are given as (1) Itukapiri; (2) Opu-Okongo; (3) Kala-Okongo; (4) Okolobirianga; (5) Finikono-wei-ama; (6) Onyakiama; (7) Kolomaniama; (8) Inkundi-ama; (9) Elele-ama; (10) Agbala-ama; (11) Okpopiri; (12) Amanyanaboamagho-biobaragha; (13) Bogomukoroama (now Ikirikakubu); (14) Odioma.

APPENDIX II

GENEALOGY OF THE KINGS OF NEMBE

The succession of kings was determined by the matrilineal principle that a child belongs to the mother's family and inherits on the mother's line. For this reason kings and chiefs invariably married women from the neighboring clans by "big dowry" (see Kay Williamson, Changes in the Marriage System of the Okrika Ijo, *Africa*, XXXII, No. 1 [Jan. 1962], 53–64). No Nembe chief or important person would normally allow his daughter to be married by big dowry since by the process the woman lost to her husband her rights over issues of the marriage. By marrying women outside their own people, and by big dowry, the kings ensured that their children would be eligible to succeed them in office. Ladies of the royal line were of course married to chiefs in Nembe, and their own children thus remained in the line of succession. The genealogical tree (see next page) for Ogbolomabiri is well marked from Ogio. The earlier kings may have been, in the main, sons or brothers of their predecessors. The parentage of Ogio himself is not known.

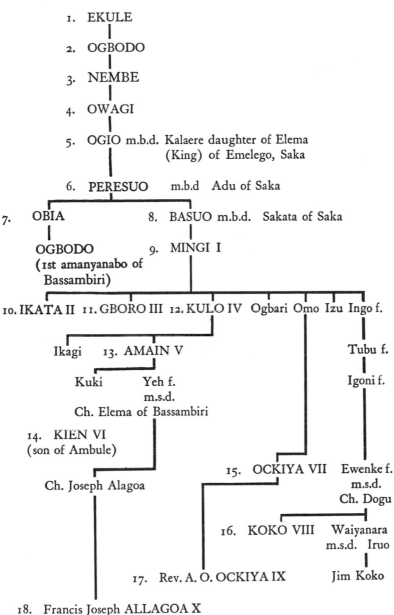

1. EKULE

2. OGBODO

3. NEMBE

4. OWAGI

5. OGIO m.b.d. Kalaere daughter of Elema
   (King) of Emelego, Saka

6. PERESUO   m.b.d   Adu of Saka

7. OBIA   8. BASUO m.b.d. Sakata of Saka

   OGBODO   9. MINGI I
   (1st amanyanabo of
   Bassambiri)

10. IKATA II 11. GBORO III 12. KULO IV Ogbari Omo Izu Ingo f.

   Ikagi   13. AMAIN V   Tubu f.

   Kuki   Yeh f.   Igoni f.
               m.s.d.
   Ch. Elema of Bassambiri

14. KIEN VI
(son of Ambule)

                               15. OCKIYA VII   Ewenke f.
   Ch. Joseph Alagoa   m.s.d.
                                                Ch. Dogu

                       16. KOKO VIII Waiyanara
                                      m.s.d. Iruo

        17. Rev. A. O. OCKIYA IX   Jim Koko

18. Francis Joseph ALLAGOA X

   m.b.d. = married big dowry
   f.   = female
   m.s.d. = married small dowry

APPENDIX III

FRAGMENTS OF THE COMEY TREATY OF 1856

Article 1.

"That the Kings and Chiefs of the countries connected in trade with the Rio Bento duly appreciating the benefit of legitimate traffic, hereby guarantee that from this date forward they shall not engage in or sanction the exportation of slaves from this country.

Article 2

"That the comey of vessels entering the river for the purpose of trade be for vessels of two masts to pay two puncheons worth of goods; vessels of three masts to pay three puncheons worth of goods to each King [Kiya of Obullambry and Arishma of Bassambry], that boats or vessels coming here with cargo and bringing no produce away are to be excepted and that for each ship taking part produce out of the river as tenderage to complete her cargo elsewhere, the comey to be five bars for each cask.

Article 7

"That the comey and pilotage being paid no other tax or payment is to be demanded under any pretence whatever. Water is not to be refused in the pilots' town called Twaw, nor is any demand to be made for the privilege of watering. Ground for the erection of houses and for the storing of casks and goods is to be granted free of all charges, and it is considered, whilst in the occupation of any British subject, as British property, and the occupant for the time being is authorized to expel trespassers and to maintain his right of occupancy, and to defend himself and property against any unlawful aggression.

Article 19

"That a copy of this treaty be furnished to each chief receiving comey and a copy of that part referring to the pilotage to the Chief Pilot; the chiefs to produce it when receiving comey, and the pilot to show it to the masters upon any vessel entering the river, and that these articles be held to be the laws existing between the British supercargoes and the natives for the regulation of trade matters to be observed so long as they continue law by those who are not present at their enactment as by those who were."

Note: These articles were taken from the Nigeria Gazette of June 11, 1914, p. 972, reproducing the judgment of the Privy Council Appeal No. 54 of 1913 — Chief Young Dede and another (Appellants) versus the African Association, Limited (Respondents).

APPENDIX IV

AGREEMENT WITH THE BRASS TRADING COMPANY, 1899

"MEMORANDUM of an Agreement entered into between James Churchill Backhouse authorized by powers of Attorney to act for and on behalf of Jonathan Cockin Holt and Robert Longstaff Holt both of the city of Liverpool, Merchants carrying on business in Brass under the name or style of the Brass Trading Company of the first part and the Chiefs of the Native Council of Brass of the second part.

"Whereas the said parties of the first part have bought from Thomas Welsh and Company of Liverpool the land and premises known by the name of Senegal Company's Beach, lately bought by Thomas Welsh and Company from the African Direct Telegraph Company of London, and whereas the African Direct Telegraph Company had the land comprised in the said Senegal Company Beach on lease from the Native Chiefs of Brass, subject to an annual payment of Twenty-five pounds per annum for the free and unrestricted use and employment of the said piece of land, now this indenture witnesseth.

"1. That the Chiefs of Brass do hereby agree to the transfer of the land known as the Senegal Company's Beach from the African Direct Telegraph Company, to Thomas Welsh and Company and from the Thomas Welsh and Company to Jonathan Cockin Holt and Robert Longstaff Holt trading in Brass under the style of the Brass Trading Company their heirs, executors or assigns to be used by them for such purposes as they may deem convenient, without restriction, reservation or encumbrance, together with foreshore thereof with free access to the river in front of said land and with the right to construct and make use of any houses, buildings, Wharfs, Jetties or other structures thereon.

"2. That the said parties of the first part shall pay to the Chiefs of Brass or their legal representatives the sum of Twenty-five pounds of sterling per annum payable quarterly on the first of January, first of April, first of July and first of October of each year.

"3. The Chiefs of Brass hereby convenant with the said Jonathan Cockin Holt and Robert Longstaff Holt their Heirs executors and assigns that the said land is hereby secured to their use enjoyment and disposal in perpetuity subject always to the rent agreed upon and expressed in the preceeding clause.

"Dated in Brass Twenty-fifth day of November, 1899.

"James Churchill Backhouse for and on behalf of the Brass Trading Company.	Chief Nathaniel Hardstone on behalf of the Native Council	His X Mark
"Two 2/6 d stamps.	Signed in my presence this twenty-fifth day of November, 1899. (Sgd.) R. Eranvill A. D. C. Brass	

"One 2/6 d stamp Register here at Brass.
    25th November, 1899

(Sgd.) R. Eranvill A. D. C. Brass."

APPENDIX V

ATTENDANCE LIST OF MEMBERS OF
THE COURT OF EQUITY, BRASS RIVER (1884–89)

10th June 1884	James Tasker Peter de Cardi C. J. Townsend J. F. Hughes	Chairman
3rd July 1884	James Tasker C. J. Townsend John Hughes	Chairman
17th November 1884	James Tasker J.,F. Hughes John H. Swainson	in Chair Term as Postmaster and Chairman — 3 months ended Elected Chairman
17th January 1885	James Tasker John MacArthur William H. Young John H. Swainson	Chairman
4th February 1885	James Tasker John MacArthur W. H. Young John H. Swainson	Chairman

19th August 1885	A. Sohucke C. J. Townsend T. P. Williams J. Swainson	Chairman
30th September 1885	A. Sohucke C. J. Townsend Williams Swainson	

Also in attendance:
Craigie of H.M.S. "Flirt"
King and Chiefs of Brass

King Abeefa	Chief Koko
Chief Doggu	Chief Spiff
Chief Kemmer	Chief Carrie
Chief Allagugu	Chief Sambo
Chief Cameroons	Chief Deddy
Chief Hacido	Chief Warry
Chief Rainbow	Chief Smoke
Chief Abedy	

2nd October 1885	A. Sohucke T. P. Williams C. J. Townsend Baker	Chairman
9th October 1885	Signatories to Craigie Declaration:	
	C. J. Townsend	Agent for Messrs. Hatton & Cookson
	Chas. Baker	Agent for Messrs. John Lander & Co.
	Arthur Sohucke	Agent for Messrs. Thos. Harrison & Co.
	Thos. B. Williams	(Rio Bento Kernel Co.)
7th November 1885	Arthur Sohucke	Agent for Messrs. Thos. Harrison & Co.
	Chas. Baker	Agent for Messrs. John Lander & Co.
	I. R. T. Thwaites	Agent for Messrs. Stewart & Douglas

W. E. Jinks   Agent for Messrs. G. A.
                              Moore & Co.

C. J. Townsend   Agent for Messrs. Hat-
                              ton & Cookson

ATTENDANCE LIST OF MEMBERS OF
THE GOVERNING COUNCIL FOR BRASS RIVER

26th November   1st   Meeting,   H.B.M.
1887   Consul was permanent
                                           President
          C. J. Townsend   Vice President
          A. A. Whitehouse
          J. H. Swainson
          J. S. Cockburn
          T. J. Davis
          Chief W. H. Kemmer
          Chief Samuel Sambo
          Chief Jacob Cameroon
          Chief Dogu
          Chief Smoke
          D. E. Jinks   Clerk of the Council

2nd December   2nd Meeting
1887   C. J. Townsend   Vice President
          J. H. Swainson
          T. J. Davis
          Chief W. H. Kemmer
          Chief Sambo
          Chief Cameroon
          Chief Dogu
          Chief Smoke
          W. E. Jinks   Clerk of the Council

7th December   3rd Meeting
1887   Harry Johnston   President, Acting Con-
          C. de Cardi   sul
          C. J. Townsend
          W. E. Jinks
          A. A. Whitehouse
          J. S. Cockburn

J. H. Swainson
J. Tasker
Chief Kemmer
Chief Sambo
Chief Cameroon

Also present:

Admiral Greebee   Chief Ecedi
Chief Egebta   Chief Dogu'
Chief Spiff

23rd December 1887		5th Meeting

C. J. Townsend
C. de Cardi
A. A. Whitehouse
W. H. Inglish
Thos. Davies
Chief Cameroon
Chief Dogu
Chief Smoke
Chief Kemmer
Chief Sambo
W. E. Jinks   Clerk of the Council

20th January 1888		9th Meeting

C. J. Townsend
C. de Cardi
James Tasker
Rev. John Robinson
Chief Cameroon
W. E. Jinks

12th March 1888		16th Meeting
		Acting Consul

H. H. Johnston
C. J. Townsend
A. A. Whitehouse
C. de Cardi
W. E. Jinks
Thos. Davies
Chief Smoke
Chief Cameroon
Chief Kemmer
Chief Dogu
Chief Sambo

Also present:
Cap. Harrison of H.M.S. "Bramble"

Chief Dedy	Chief Nangiby
Chief Egbeta	Chief Opomah
Chief Gourkoma	Chief Bokolo

23rd March
1888

    A. A. Whitehouse
    E. J. Pridden
    W. E. Jinks
    Archdeacon Crowther
    Chief Cameroon

18th Meeting

5th May
1888

    Townsend
    C. de Cardi
    Geo. Mardock
    Rev. John Robinson
    W. E. Jinks
    Archdeacon Crowther
    Thos. Davies
    Chief Kemmer

23rd Meeting

19th May
1888

    Townsend
    Rev. J. Robinson
    Chief Cameroons
    C. C. McGarvir

Special meeting

(in place of Cockburn for Stewart and Douglas)

    G. Mardock

Clerk

6th April
1889

35th and last recorded meeting

    A. A. Whitehouse
    C. C. McGarvie

Acting Vice President

Also present:
Chiefs of the O'Bullambry side:

James Spiff	Dogo
George Ockia	Egabee
Robert Egbeta	Ujulu
Dedi	William Kemmer
Imbiabugo	

Chief Frederick William Koko presented as King

Note. The names of Chiefs given in the above list should read as follows:

King Abeefa	= King Ebifa of Bassambiri
Chief Doggu, Dogo	= Chief Dogu, father of King Koko, Mingi VIII
Chief Allagugu	= Chief Joseph Alagoa, father of Mingi X.
Chief Hacido, Ecedi	= Chief Shidi of Twon.
Chief Abedy	= Chief Abedi of Bassambiri. Died 1895 during Akassa War.
Chief Carrie	= Chief Kari.
Chief Deddy, Dedy, Dedi	= Chief Dede.
Chief Warry	= Chief Warri (Iwowari).
Chief Smoke	= Chief Felix Amabebe Smoke of Pegi House, Bassambiri.
Chief Gourkoma	= Chief Guokuma, brother and successor of Ebifa as head of Duguruyai House, Bassambiri.
Chief Nangiby	= Chief Inengite.
Chief Opomah	= Chief Epemu of Bassambiri.
Chief Imbiabugo	= Chief Bugo of Bassambiri.
Chief Egabee	= Chief Egebe of Ogbolomabiri.
Chief Ujulu	= Chief Izulu of Oglomabiri.

APPENDIX VI

HOUSE RULE PROCLAMATION AND AMENDMENT

Proclamation No. 26 — 1901
(Enacted 21st November, 1901)

WHEREAS it is expedient for the preservation of peace and good order in the Protectorate to make provision for the maintenance of the authority vested in Heads of Houses by Native law and custom:

BE IT THEREFORE ENACTED as follows:—

Short title.

1. This Proclamation may be cited as "The Native House Rule Proclamation, 1901."

Definitions.

2. In this proclamation, unless the context otherwise requires,

"House" means a group of persons subject by Native law and custom to the control, authority, and rule of a chief, known as a Head of a House.

"Member of a House" means and includes any person who by birth or in any other manner is or becomes subject to the control, authority, and rule of a Head of a House.

"Native Law and Customs" includes any Native Law and Custom existing in the Protectorate relating to Houses, not repugnant to natural justice, nor incompatible either directly or by necessary implication with any Proclamation in force at the commencement of this Proclamation, or which may thereafter come into operation, and any regulations relating to Houses passed under the provisions of "The Native Courts Proclamation, 1901," by a Native Council with the consent of the High Commissioner.

"Court" means a District Court or Native Court.

"Commissioner" means a District Commissioner holding a judicial warrant.

All members of Houses to be subject to native law and custom. Proceedings to be commenced before a commissioner.

3. Every member of a House shall from and after the commencement of this Proclamation be subject to Native Law and Custom.

4. All proceedings under this Proclamation shall be commenced before a Commissioner, who shall have full jurisdiction to determine summarily all such proceedings. Every such Commissioner may at any stage of any proceedings direct the same to be transferred to and determined by any Native Court in his district, unless one of the parties to such proceedings is a European.

Offences by members of Houses against law relating to Houses. Penalty.

5. Every member of a House who refuses or neglects to submit himself to the control, authority, and rule of the Head of his House in accordance with Native law and custom shall be liable on conviction to a fine not exceeding £50, or to imprisonment with or without hard labour for any term not exceeding one year, or to both.

Warrant for arrest of member of House committing an offence.

6. Where a member of a House is charged upon oath of the Head of the House or his representative with an offence under the last preceding section, the Commissioner before whom the charge is made may issue a warrant directing the person named therein to arrest and bring before him such member of the House to be dealt with for the offence with which he is charged.

Offence by head of House against law relating to Houses.

7. Every Head of a House who neglects or refuses to perform, or acts in contravention of, the obligations imposed upon him by the Native law and customs towards any member or members of his house shall be liable on conviction to a

Penalty.

fine not exceeding £50, or to imprisonment with or without hard labour for any term not exceeding one year, or to both.

Wandering members of Houses and destitute persons.

8. Any person wandering abroad or having no apparent means of subsistence may be arrested by any officer of any Court within the district in which such person is found, without a warrant, and brought before the Commissioner of such district, and questioned as to his means of subsistence and to which House he belongs.

If it appears that he belongs to a House, notice shall be given to the Head of such House who may thereupon commence such proceedings as he think fit under this Proclamation, or under Native law and custom.

If the person arrested refuses when questioned to answer to the satisfaction of the Commissioner, and it does not appear that he belongs to a House, or if the Head of the House to whom any notice of the arrest has been given as aforesaid does not commence proceedings within seven days after the receipt of such notice, such person, unless he proves that he has sufficient means of subsistence, or that his want of such means is not the result of his own fault, shall be liable to imprisonment with hard labour for any term not exceeding one year.

Power of court to order —

9. In any proceedings under this Proclamation the Court, whether it impose a fine or term of imprisonment or not, may order:

Payment of compensation;

(i) That the defendant pay to the complainant such sum as the Court may think fit as compensation for any loss or injury sustained.

Discharge from obligations;

(ii) That upon payment of such sum or fulfillment of such conditions as the Court may direct, or unconditionally, the complainant or defendant be discharged from further performance of all or part of the obligations imposed upon him by Native law and custom relating to houses; or

Fulfillment of terms of settlement.

(iii) That the terms of any arrangement agreed to by the parties for the settlement of any question with respect to their obligations under Native law and custom relating to houses be carried into effect.

Any person who shall commit a breach of any order under this section shall be liable to imprisonment with or without hard labour for any term not exceeding six months.

Penalty for resisting arrest.

10. Every person who resists or obstructs the lawful apprehension of himself for any offence under this Proclamation, or escapes or attempts to escape from any custody in which he is lawfully detained, shall be liable to a fine not exceeding £50, or to imprisonment with or without hard labour for any term not exceeding one year, or to both.

Offences by employers in respect of members of Houses.

11. Any European or Native (1) who knowing a Native to be a member of a House employs such Native without the express or implied consent of the Head of the House, or (2) who not knowing that a Native is a member of a House, does not use every endeavour to ascertain whether such Native is or is not a member of a House before employing such Native, or (3) who not knowing, notwithstanding that he has used every endeavour, that a Native is a member of a House employs such Native, and subsequently discovering that he is a member of a House fails to give notice of the fact to the Head of the House to which such Native belongs, shall be liable to a

Penalty.

fine not exceeding £50, or to imprisonment with or without hard labour for any term not exceeding one year, or to both.

Payment of expenses and compensation for arrest.

12. (1) The Court may order any person convicted of an offence under this Proclamation to pay all or any part of the costs and expenses of the proceedings against him; and

(2) Where it appears to the Court that any proceedings are malicious, vexatious, or frivolous,

the Court may order the complainant to pay all or any part of the costs and expenses of the accused, and where the accused has been arrested on a charge on the oath of the complainant may order the complainant to pay in addition to any such costs and expenses, or any of them, such sum not exceeding £25, as it may think fit, as compensation.

Imprisonment in default of payment.

13. The Court may at any time direct that payment of the costs and expenses and compensation, or any of them, ordered to be paid under the provisions of the last preceding section, shall be made on or before a specified date, and may also order that if default is made in such payment the person so directed to pay shall be imprisoned with or without hard labour for any term not exceeding three months, unless payment of such costs, expenses, and compensation or any of them ordered to be paid, be sooner made.

Imprisonment not to extinguish liability.

14. No imprisonment under the provisions of this Proclamation shall operate as a satisfaction or extinguishment of any liability to pay any sum ordered by the Court to be paid as costs, expenses or compensation, under the provisions of this Proclamation.

Commencement of Proclamation.

15. This Proclamation shall commence and come into operation on the first day of January, in the year of Our Lord One thousand nine hundred and two.

No. 1   1912

COLONY OF SOUTHERN NIGERIA

An Ordinance to Amend the Native House Rule Ordinance
(8th February, 1912)

BE IT ENACTED by the Governor of the Colony of Southern Nigeria with the advice and consent of the Legislative Council thereof as follows:—

Short title.

1. This Ordinance may be cited as the Native House Rule (Amendment) Ordinance, 1912.

Terms on which members may leave their House.

2. The Native House Rule Ordinance is hereby amended as follows:—

(1) The following section is inserted after section four —

5. Any Member of a House may apply to the Commissioner of the District to fix an amount upon payment of which he shall cease to be a Member of his House and be freed from all the obligations imposed upon him by Native Law and Custom relating to Houses. The Commissioner shall thereupon fix the amount to be paid and decree his immediate discharge from such liabilities either:

(a) On payment of the aforesaid amount or
(b) On his giving security to the satisfaction of the Commissioner for payment by annual instalments spread over not more than three years.

The payment or payments shall be made to the District Commissioner, and paid out by him. A Member of a House shall, on ceasing to be a Member, forfeit every claim and privilege of Membership of the House including that of part ownership of property real and personal but shall be entitled to retain and remove all his own personal property.

The sum payable may not exceed the maximum amount fixed by the Provincial Commissioner for each House, which sum shall in no case be greater than £50, and in the case of persons of the labouring class or canoe boys shall not exceed £15.

(2) By inserting in section nine of the principal Ordinance between the words 'Ordinance' and 'Court' the words "save and except in proceedings under section 5 of this Ordinance."

(3) Sections five, six, seven, eight, nine, ten, eleven, twelve, thirteen, and fourteen are hereby re-numbered six, seven, eight, nine, ten, eleven, twelve, thirteen, fourteen, and fifteen respectively.

Passed in the Legislative Council this 8th day of February, in the year of our Lord one thousand nine hundred and twelve.

APPENDIX VII

LIST OF "CONSULS," 1849–1929

Consuls for the Bight of Biafra (Fernando Po)
- 1853   J. Beecroft
- 1855   T. J. Hutchinson
- 1861   Capt. R. F. Burton
- 1864   C. Livingstone

Consuls for the Bights of Benin and Biafra
- 1867   C. Livingstone
- 1873   C. Hartley
- 1878   D. Hopkins
- 1880   E. H. Hewett

Commissioners and Consuls General for the Oil Rivers and Niger Coast Protectorate (Calabar)
- 1891   Major C. M. MacDonald
- 1896   R. D. R. Moore

Administrative Officers at Brass Consulate

1891	Major C. M. MacDonald	Vice-Consul
1892	E. E. Dunn	Ac. Vice-Consul
1894	Mr. Harper Moore	Vice-Consul
1895	Mr. Harper Moore	Vice-Consul
	Mr. Cuthbert E. Harrison	Ac. Vice-Consul
1896	Capt. Gallwey	Ac. Vice-Consul
	C. E. Harrison	Vice-Consul

1897	W. F. W. Fosbery	Ac. Vice-Consul
	A. G. Leonard	Vice-Consul
1899	R. Eranvill	Asst. District Commissioner
1902	Reginald Arthur Roberts	District Commissioner
1903		
1905	A. R. E. Holt D. O.	Capt. F. M. Leigh-Lye, A.D.O.
	F. O. M. Cheke, D. O.	Capt. F. M. Leigh-Lye A.D.L.
1906	Major W. A. C. Cockburn	P. H. A. Grant, A.D.O.
1907	A. R. E. Holt	J. M. Pollen, A.D.O.
1908	D. E. Price	J. M. Pollen
	H. S. Gladstone	Capt. Gervaise Lyons
		Capt. F. Sinclair
1909	Capt. F. Sinclair, Ac. D. O.	
	J. M. Pinder	P. J. Gardner
	Capt. F. Sinclair	
1910	Capt. F. Sinclair	E. C. Palmer, A.D.O.
	A. D. Horden	
1911	A. D. Horden	M. Maclaren
	F. Sinclair	
1912	F. Sinclair	G. K. Given
	G. K. Given, Ac. D. O.	
	A. D. Horden	
	F. Sinclair	
1913	F. Sinclair	M. D. H. Lyon
	G. K. Given, Ac. D. O.	G. K. Given
1914	G. K. Given, Ac. D. O.	
	G. N. Hopkins	
1915	G. N. Hopkins	
	F. M. Leigh-Lye	
	Capt. E. B. Wauton	
1916	Capt. E. B. Wauton	
1917	Capt. E. B. Wauton	
	C. D. Blayney, Ac. D. O.	
1918	C. D. Blayney	
1919	C. D. Blayney	
	A. W. Nolan	
	G. N. Heathcott	
1920	Capt. E. B. Wauton	
1921	E. B. Wauton	
	M. D. H. Lyon	
1922	M. D. H. Lyon	
	Harry Maddocks	
	H. N. Cleverly	

1923	H. N. Cleverly	
	M. D. H. Lyon	
	K. A. B. Cochrane	
1924	K. A. B. Cochrane	
	I. W. E. Dods	
1925	I. W. E. Dods	
	Capt. John Ashley	
1926	Capt. John Ashley	
	H. Maddocks	
1927	H. Maddocks	
	Capt. J. Ashley	R. S. Mallinson, A.D.O.
1928	Capt. J. Ashley	R. S. Mallinson
	Capt. J. N. Hill	
1929	Capt. J. N. Hill	
	J. C. Porter	

APPENDIX VIII

THE BAR AS AN ACCOUNTING UNIT

Exchange rates of the bar effective from Jan. 7, 1886

Big cargo

5 cases gin equals	⅛	bar
5 kegs gun powder	⅖	"
5 guns	⅖	"
5 demijohns	⅛	"

Small cargo

5 ps. madras equals	⅛	bar
3 ps. silk	⅖	"
5 bags rice	⅘	"
40 matchets	⅛	"
10 bags shot	⅛	"
1 ps. flannel	⅛	"
2 Snider rifles	⅛	"
32 iron bars	⅛	"
40 gallons pots	⅛	"

"Bar for kernels" rates, effective February 1, 1886

24 ps. madras equals	1 puncheon kernels		
15 matchets	⅛	"	"
15 one gallon pots	⅛	"	"
1 ps. silk	⅛	"	"
5 bags shot	⅛	"	"
8 cases gin and 8 ps. madras	1	"	"
1 hogs head tobacco	14	"	"
35 heads tobacco	⅛	"	"
1 base pipes	4 ps. madras		

1 bag rice	4 ps. madras
1 case gin	4 ps. madras

All other small cargo at the rate of £2: 10:–d per puncheon.

"Bar for oil" rates, effective February 15, 1886

Big Cargo

4 cases gin equals	1/8	puncheon	oil
4 demijohns	1/8	"	"
2 guns	1/8	"	"
2 powder	1/8	"	"

Small cargo

4 ps. madras equals	1/8	puncheon	oil
1 ps. silk	1/8	"	"
1 box pipes	1/8	"	"
1 bag rice	1/8	"	"
32 matchets	8	"	"
8 bags shot	1/8	"	"
1 Snider rifle	2/8	"	"
1 ps. flannel	1/8	"	"
24 iron bars	1/8	"	"
3 gallon pots	1/8	"	"

Cash puncheon oil: half big, half small cargo. Workbar *Chiefs* 1/8 puncheon small cargo per puncheon. *Boys* 3 ps. madras per puncheon. *Tobacco* for 1 Hogshead Tobacco 6 puncheons clear oil, no workbar. Topside rate.

Other small cargo, not mentioned at the rate of 5 per puncheon.

Workbar was the bonus paid to chiefs and their boys on produce brought for sale.

Topside was the percentage of a minor chief's profits the supercargo retained for the head of the subchief's House.

Note: These tables were taken from the Proceedings of the Court of Equity, Brass River 1883–91, at the National Archives of Nigeria, Ibadan.

NOTES

CHAPTER 1

1. K. Onwuka Dike, *Trade and Politics in the Niger Delta, 1830–1885* (London, 1956), pp. 30–31.

2. For a discussion of origins and chronology, see Chapters 3 and 4.

3. Adebiyi Tepowa, "A Short History of Brass and Its People," in the *Journal of the African Society* (now *African Affairs*), 1907. Tepowa signed himself District Clerk, Political Department, Southern Nigeria.

4. Percy Amaury Talbot, *The Peoples of Southern Nigeria*, 4 vols. (London, 1926); Arthur Glyn Leonard, *The Lower Niger and Its Tribes* (London, 1906); K. O. Dike, *op. cit.*

5. William Balfour Baikie, *Narrative of an Exploring Voyage up the River Kworra and Binue (commonly known as the Niger and Tsadda) in 1854* (London, 1856), p. 427.

6. The place name and the fishing trap are differentiated by tone. The trap consisted of a low fence across a mangrove swamp at ebb tide. When the tide came in it overflowed the fence and the fish would go in. At the following ebb tide, many of the fish stayed behind too late to pass over the fence. These were picked up by the fishermen or women.

7. Sir John Kirk, *Report on the Disturbances at Brass*, Appendix E, "Names of Towns and Villages in the Nimbe District (including the whole known as Brass)," pp. 11–12, Africa No. 3 (1896) [C. 7977].

8. NA/E, Onprof 1/16/34, File No. OP 527/1915, "Provinces and Divisions of the Colony and Southern Provinces of the Protectorate [of Nigeria]."

These census figures cannot be taken as being completely accurate. The first Nigerian "census" was that of 1911 and has been described officially as "mainly estimate." P. A. Talbot, who was census officer in 1921, has suggested that an allowance of 5 per cent error be made in his figures for townships and a 10 per cent addition may safely be made for the tribal count. The figures for Brass Division fell under Talbot's last category. The census officer for the Southern Provinces in the 1931 census, Mr. H. B. Cox, complained that his work was interrupted by the 1929 riots in Eastern Nigeria, and that afterwards it was attended with little cooperation from the people. The affair "finally became a mere compilation of existing data, and the results have, often, only a provisional character." The 1953 census was misunderstood to be a taxation measure and many people refused to show up for a count.

9. The term "tribe" as used here follows Talbot's description of it as an ethnic group speaking the same language, having the same customs and religion, and claiming a common descent. The Ijaw clan represents a subgroup with a distinctive dialect and, to the east of Brass, often organized as a city-state, but not so organized to the west.

10. Both Eastern and Western Ijaw, as terms used here, are areas that lie to the west of Brass. The Eastern Ijaw are so called because they form part of Brass Division and are in Eastern Nigeria. The Western Ijaw are in Western Nigeria.

11. A. F. C. Ryder, "An Early Portuguese Trading Voyage to the Forcados River," in *Journal of the Historical Society of Nigeria*, i, No. 4 (December 1959), 296.

12. Baikie, *Narrative of an Exploring Voyage . . .*, p. 40.

13. NA/E, Owdist 1/9/35, Letter No. 81/38/1929 of Jan. 31, K. A. B. Cochrane, D.O., to the Resident, Owerri Province. The following towns are listed as Oru: Elele, Egwe, Ozara, Ama, Amago, Omoma, Aji, Uli, Akatta, Awka, Oboro, Mbidi, Oteru, Ibi, Akoma, Nempi, and Awa Mama. "The people of all towns claiming to be Oru say that they are the children of Awma. They claim to be closely related to the Egbema clan of the Ahoada Division, Ogu Ali Ocha in Onitsha, and Egwe and Ebu in Owerri." There is no evident connection between the Ibo Oru and the Ijaw Oru of Dr. Baikie.

14. A. G. Leonard, *The Lower Niger and Its Tribes*, p. 18.

15. Talbot, *The Peoples of Southern Nigeria*, IV, 72.

16. The 1931 census gave the Ijaw a total population of 156,324 in the Southern Provinces, and distributed among the Provinces as follows: Lagos Colony, 1,341; the Cameroons, 1,268; Ondo Province, 7,039; Owerri Province, 113,219; Warri Province, 32,651; Onitsha, 279; Benin, 485; Calabar, 22; and Ogoja, 20.

17. Dietrich Westermann and M. A. Bryan, *Languages of West Africa, Handbook of African Languages*, Part II (London, 1952) pp. 121–22.

18. J. H. Greenberg, *Studies in African Linguistic Classification* (New Haven, 1955), p. 8.

19. Leonard, *op. cit.*, p. 28. "Taking the Ijo language next, a comparison between it and the Ibani, Okrika, New Calabar and Brass dialects reveals the fact that all four of them, also Oru, are dialects of the Ijaw."

Hans Wolff, "Niger Delta Languages: Classification," in *Anthropological Linguistics*, 1, No. 8 (November 1959). Dr. Wolff refers to the dialects as "languages," and classifies them under Greenberg's Ijaw sub-family of Niger Congo languages.

CHAPTER 2

1. C. N. de Cardi, "A Short description of the Natives of the Niger Coast Protectorate, with some Account of their Customs, Religion, Trade, etc.," Appendix I in Mary H. Kingsley, *West African Studies* (London 1899), pp. 443–566. Miss Kingsley described de Cardi as a man with "unrivalled knowledge of the natives of the Niger Delta." By his own accounts, he had been connected with West Africa from 1862–96 and made a special study of domestic slavery in the Nembe area, "where it was carried on with less hardship to the slaves themselves than any place else in the Delta." (p. 471).

2. De Cardi in Mary Kingsley, *op. cit.*, p. 475.

3. Proclamation No. 26, enacted Nov. 21, 1901, effective from Jan. 1, 1902.

4. See Southern Nigeria Despatches no. 241 of May 24, 1913, Lugard to Harcourt, Secretary of State; No. 489 of July 21, 1913, Harcourt to Lugard; and No. 541 of August 9, 1913, Harcourt to Lugard.

5. NA/E, Records of the Secretariat, Enugu, File No. C.230/13. The following petitions are included: Chief Dore Numa and others for the Jekri Chiefs and Sobos, March 18, 1914; Chief Nathaniel Yekorogha, Ben Warri, Joseph Alagoa, Thomas Abayeh, Neck, Isaac W. Sambo, etc., for Brass Chiefs, May 26, 1914; Chiefs of Degema, Okrika, Bonny, and Opobo jointly, June 29, 1914; and Obon and Chiefs of Calabar, July 8, 1914.

6. NA/E, Records of the District Office, Brass, File No. W.597/1920, Petition by Chiefs Alagoa, Bokolo, and twenty-eight others to the Governor.

7. NA/E, Brassdist, File No. BR.642, pp. 82–84. The old chief had written to the district officer through the amanyanabo, "Have my son sit in the Court, and I will die happy. . . ."

8. NA/E, Brassdist, File No. BR.861, p. 192, letter from Olukutu A. Amain, C. Mendie Kien, and J. A. Alagoa to Resident, Owerri Province,

Sept. 26, 1940. The late J. A. Alagoa, the author's father, was deputy chief of the Alagoa House.

9. Francis O. J. Alagoa was then a magistrate at Port Harcourt, and arrived dramatically at the nick of time to deliver his victory address.

10. NA/E, Brassdist, File No. 44. The reconciliation was effected before the A.D.O., Mr. A. F. F. P. Newns, and Mr. I. A, Olali, Interpreter.

11. This account was given by Chief Captain I. Peresuo in a petition to the A.D.O., Brass, dated Sept. 19, 1938.

12. Rev. D. O. Ockiya, "History of Nembe," n. d., MS. Tepowa, "A Short History of Brass," *Journal of the African Society*, 1907, p. 37, n. 3. Few details of the operation of Ibidi are now remembered.

13. Tepowa, p. 63.

14. Material in this section is taken from Ockiya, *op. cit.*, Tepowa, *op. cit.*, and Capt. E. B. Wauton, Intelligence Reports in NA/E Brasdist and Degdist.

15. According to Mr. J. S. Berena of Okpoma, it is also called Ada or Adagba. He believes the word to mean "the big sword," *ada*, sword, and *agba*, big. The name Adagba was later given to the boa constrictor, which is worshipped along with the python.

16. NA/E, Brassdist.

17. R. and J. Lander, *Journal of an Expedition to Explore the Course and Termination of the Niger with a Narrative of a Voyage Down that River to Its Termination* (London, 1834), II, 268.

18. NA/E, Brassdist, File No. BR.351, vol. I. In a letter, Anthony Ockiya to Major H. Webber, dated Oct. 16, 1930. A list of chiefs and the shares given to them in 1928–29 follows. The story of the ivory is also in this file.

A. O. OCKIYA (amanyanabo)	£ 20	: —	: —
Chief Joseph Alagoa	3	: —	: —
Chiefs of Okpoma and Twon	5	: —	: —
Chief Natebo	1	: —	: —
Chief Iboama-Igbeta	1	: 15	: —
Chief Koko	1	: 5	: —
Chief Bugo	—	: 6	: —
Chief Amangi	—	: 10	: —
Chief Gam-Dede	1	: 5	: —
Chief Ockiya-Berena	2	: 10	: —
Chief Oruwari	1	: 5	: —
Chief Karitongha	1	: 5	: —
Chief Ogbari	1	: 5	: —
Chief Peresuo	—	: 8	: —
Chief Ougha	—	: 12	: —

19. NA/E, Brassdist, File No. BR. 57.

20. O. Ukelonu, *Report of the Commission of Inquiry into the Nembe Chieftaincy Dispute*, Official Document No. 24, 1960, Government Printer, Enugu.

21. For an account of the civil war, see Chapter 4.

22. A. Tepowa, *op. cit.*, chapters VI–VII, and pp. 55–59.

23. NA/E, Brassdist.

24. De Cardi in Mary Kingsley, *op. cit.*, pp. 484–87.

25. Cited by Rev. D. O. Ockiya.

26. A. Tepowa, *op. cit.*, pp. 58–59.

27. K. O. Dike, *Trade and Politics in the Niger Delta, 1830–1885* (London, 1956), p. 31.

28. K. O. Dike, *op. cit.*, p. 33.

CHAPTER 3

1. At informal gatherings — at parties, meetings, by night around the family fireside or outdoors by moonlight — opportunities are taken for recounting episodes in traditional history. Information may be given in the form of songs, riddles (*du*), fables (*lugu*), or myth. See Jan Vansina, "Recording the oral history of the Bakuba — I. Methods," in *Journal of African History*, 1, No. 1 (1960).

2. A. Tepowa, "A Short History of Brass and Its People," pp. 33–40.

3. Tepowa, p. 32.

4. Onyoma has left a deeper imprint on the minds of the people, and it is mentioned more often in songs and riddle. One such riddle runs as follows:

Q. *Onyoma amanyanaowei tei eke amene ta warinyana aramatin?* — "By what pet name does the King of Onyoma call his head wife?"

A. *Gbin oduguru, gbin warikubu.* — "She who makes a resounding din with her heels on the ground as she bustles into the room and out into the parlour." (Literally, *Gbin* the room, *Gbin* the parlour).

5. A. Tepowa, *op. cit.*, p. 36. Tepowa translates this, "Onyoama, yam is sweeter than fish, yam and fish are equally sweet, go and enquire the reason of the palaver why my father killed my husband, as I am going to Kula." He has mistaken the phrase *gbori pele* to mean "the same sweetness," and translated it "equally sweet." It should read "the same pot" — "Onyoama, yam is sweeter than fish, yam and fish are cooked in the same pot. . . ." The phrase "*Kula ntaba*" must be an archaism or a foreign phrase. Rev. D. O. Ockiya translates it "Prince of Kula," but it could be "people of Kula."

6. A. Tepowa, *op. cit.*, p. 37, nn 2–3. The Kula sang the following paean of victory:

"Onyoma ye ƙingerebo dibigha mi ama."
Tepowa does not provide a translation, but it means "This town of Onyoma will bury more than one." Tepowa gives another Nembe proverb connected with this incident to which he provides a translation: *"Onyoma pere fua tarigha* —"Are you the king of Onyoma who hates his son-in-law?" There is again a slight mistake; it should be "The priest-king of Onyoma does not love sons-in-law."

7. P. C. Lloyd, *The Benin Kingdom* (London, 1957), p. 179.

8. A. Tepowa, *op. cit.*, pp. 39–40. King Kulo died in 1832. The meaning is that Kulo maintained peace all over the kingdom, and not that these towns were founded during King Kulo's reign.

9. Rev. D. O. Ockiya, "Autobiography," and "History of Nembe," both at the National Archives, Enugu, in MS. Rev. Daniel "Ogiriki" Ockiya (died 1954) was a son of King Constantine Ockiya (died 1879). He was old enough to take part in the 1895 Akassa War. He later became an Anglican pastor and taught and preached throughout the Brass District — opening up new missions and schools in the Ogbia and Ijaw areas. A memorial to his missionary work are the Infant Primer and the translation into the Nembe language of the Bible. In the 1920's, he had been approached with an offer of the crown. He preferred to carry on his missionary work and permitted his brother, Anthony Ockiya, to be crowned in 1926.

He checked his information for the "History" with all persons in Nembe with a reputation for knowledge of oral history, including Chief Joseph Alagoa (died 1934).

10. Rev. D. O. Ockiya, "History of Nembe," cites for the paragraph on Nuwa and Ginuwa, "Itshekiri History, Chapter XII, p. 218." Mr. Ockiya was convinced that the founders of the Ockiya House, if not the entire Nembe royal line, were of Itsekiri origin.

11. A. Tepowa, *op. cit.*, p. 37.

12. Tepowa, p. 41.

13. The only occupations mentioned in the legends are fishing, hunting, trading, and piracy. Fishing communities tend to refer to each other by the method of fishing peculiar to the group.

14. Information received from Mr. J. S. Berena, Town Clerk, Okpoma.

15. Information given by Rev. Isaac Abraham Ockiya. A starved fisherman from Fernando Po was picked up in the 1940's, having been blown across miles of ocean.

16. A. Tepowa, *op. cit.*, p. 51.

17. Another of Chief Ada Spiff's settlements — Ekperikiri — was similarly named after the local agent — Ekperi.

18. NA/E, Brassdist and Degdist. Note Intelligence Reports by E. B. Wauton and J. N. Hill.

19. NA/E, Brassdist. Two groups of Ogbia look to Oloibiri (Olei) and Abulabiri (Otokoroma), respectively, for leadership. There was little cooperation within the groups or between the two. The towns comprising the groups are

OLEI		OTOKOROMA
Oloibiri	Amurikeni	Abulabiri
Emeya	Otogidi	Imiringi
Otuasiga	Otuaka	Kolo
Waribugoama	Elebele	Anyama
Ogidiama	Otedu	Akalabagi
Otegila	Otoganaga	

20. NA/E. An Intelligence Report on the Nembe Clan in the Brass Area (Degema Division), Owerri Province, by E. N. Dickinson, A.D.O., 1932, p. 10.

21. NA/I, CSO 26, File No. 31016, Intelligence Report on the Akassa Clan, Degema Division, Owerri Province, by A. F. F. P. Newns, acting A.D.O., 1935.

22. Newns, Intelligence Report on the Akassa Clan, 1935.

23. A. G. Leonard, *The Lower Niger and Its Tribes*, p. 28.

24. Leonard, *op. cit.*, p. 23.

25. NA/E, Degdist 3/2/6. Intelligence Reports, Okrika, 1933. No author given.

Different versions were given to me by two men — Ibuluya from Okrika and Mina from Ogoloma. The exchange of ideas occurred in the newspaper, *The Eastern Star*, published at Port Harcourt, Eastern Nigeria: E. J. Alagoa, "Who are the Ijaws," July 14 and 16, 1962; Daniel Ibuluya, "Who are the Ijaws — A Rejoinder," July 25, 1962; E. T. Mina, "Who are the Ijaws — A Rejoinder to Daniel Ibuluya," August 20, 1962.

Ibuluya makes Oputibeya the first arrival and founder of Okrika and an emigrant from Amassoma in Ijaw, and states that "Opugulaya and his people who were the next to arrive or second settlers on the Okrika island came from Nembe and were settled by Oputibeya at the windward part of the island."

Mina generally agrees with the account in the text except that he states that Opu-Ogulaya came from Amassoma. He makes him a close relation of a whole series of peoples in Nembe, and also the Ijaw to the west of Nembe; "Obi, Opuogulaya's grandfather, took his children and grandchildren, including Ogien and his son Opu-Ogulaya, Okpo who founded Okpoma, Egwe who founded Egwema, Lia, who founded Liama, Kala-Ekule amongst those who founded Nembe, all in Brass, Ogbo, from whom Ogbia derived its name, Ele, wives and brothers, and established a new town, near Seibiri in Southern Ijaw, called Obiama, where Obi was king."

26. NA/E, Degist., 3/2/6. Intelligence Reports, Okrika, p. 11.

27. A. G. Leonard, *op. cit.*, p. 40. All Bonnymen who discussed the articles (see note 25 above) with me disclaimed all Ibo origin of Bonny. Ibuluya equally emphatically rejected any Ibo settlement at Okrika.

28. K. O. Dike, *Trade and Politics in the Niger Delta, 1830–1885*, p. 21. Dr. Dike considered his conclusions on migrations merely "tentative" pending the appearance of "authoritative local histories."

29. Ado was the ancient name of the Benin Empire. To the Ibo it was Ado-na-Idu. The Benin are now called the Edo tribe.

30. R. E. Bradbury, *The Benin Kingdom* (London, 1957) p. 22. Bradbury thinks that "on the east the effective boundary was the Niger. . . ."

31. William Bosman, "A New and Accurate Description of the Coast of Guinea, Letter XX of Sept. 1, 1702, from David Nyendael," in John Pinkerton, *A General Collection of the Best and Most Interesting Voyages* (London, 1814), 16, 520.

CHAPTER 4

1. K. O. Dike, *Trade and Politics in the Niger Delta, 1830–1885*, p. 23.

2. Rev. D. O. Ockiya, "History of Nembe."

3. A. Tepowa, "A Short History of Brass and Its People," p. 42.

4. Tepowa, *op. cit.*, p. 43.

5. King Ogio conducted postmortems in this square. Persons with witchcraft in their system would reveal a black clot in their inside, their intestines being dark and twisted.

6. Tepowa, *op. cit.*, p. 43.

7. Tepowa, p. 45.

8. P. A. Talbot, *Tribes of the Niger Delta* (London, 1930), p. 11. Talbot dates Amakiri's reign in Kalabari as 1770–91. This helps to date Ikata and the Bila War. Talbot, *The Peoples of Southern Nigeria*, 1, 245–51.

9. P. A. Talbot, *The Peoples of Southern Nigeria*, 1, 251. In 1791, Pepple is said to have surprised Kalabari and taken Amakiri prisoner. From that date the European ships traded more in Bonny, and Kalabari took second place to Bonny as a port.

CHAPTER 5

1. A. F. C. Ryder, "An Early Portuguese Trading Voyage to the Forcados River," *Journal of the Historical Society of Nigeria*, 1, No. 4 (Dec. 1959) 294.

2. P. A. Talbot, *The Peoples of Southern Nigeria*, I, 183, 239.

3. Talbot, *The Peoples of Southern Nigeria*, I, 34: the Strassburg Edition of Ptolemy, 1513; p. 161: Mercator, 1619, redrawn, 1925; p. 243: "A new correct map of Calibar River vulgarly called Calabar and by the Portuguese Rio Real and also of the Coast of Guinea about it, from Cape Formoso to Bonny River. Drawn very exactly on the spot in the year 1699 by several pilots jointly." From Bardot's engraving, 1766; redrawn in 1925.

4. John Barbot, *A Description of the Coasts of North and South Guinea* (Paris, 1732), p. 379. Cf. W. B. Baikie, *Narrative of an Exploring Voyage* . . ., p. 427f.

5. K. O. Dike, *Trade and Politics* . . ., p. 52.

6. Dike, *Trade and Politics* . . ., p 47. Cites Sir Richard Burton, *Wanderings in Western Africa from Liverpool to Fernando Po* (London, 1863), p. 261.

7. De Cardi in Mary Kingsley, *West African Studies*, p. 480.

8. Macgregor Laird and R. A. K. Oldfield, *Narrative of an Expedition into the Interior of Africa, by the River Niger, in the steam vessels Quorra and Alburkah in 1832, 1833 and 1834* (London 1837) I, 73.

9. J. E. Flint, *Sir George Goldie and the Making of Nigeria* (London, 1960), p. 28.

10. Sir John Kirk, *Report on the Disturbances at Brass*, p. 10.

11. Flint, *Sir George Goldie* . . ., p. 28, Letter from Ockiya and two other chiefs of Brass to Foreign Office of 7/7/76.

12. Sir William Geary, *Nigeria under British Rule* (London, 1927), p. 80. Consular report for June 30, 1856, by Thomas Hutchinson.

13. A. C. G. Hastings, *The Voyage of the Dayspring* (London, 1926), pp. 66–75.

14. K. O. Dike, *Trade and Politics* . . ., p. 101.

15. J. E. Flint, *Sir George Goldie* . . ., p. 193. The export for 1876 was estimated at 1,500 tons only.

16. Sir John Kirk, *Report on the Disturbances at Brass*, gives the high rates of customs and trade duties charged by the Company to keep away rivals.

17. W. B. Baikie, *Narrative of an Exploring Voyage* . . ., p. 356.

18. K. O. Dike, *Trade and Politics* . . ., p. 199. Cites Despatch No. 28 of August 4, 1870, Granville to Consul Livingstone.

19. Baikie, *Narrative of an Exploring Voyage* . . ., p. 317.

20. P. A. Talbot, *The Peoples of Southern Nigeria*, I, 244–45.

21. This beach was surrendered in 1926.

22. De Cardi in M. Kingsley, *West African Studies*, p. 443–47.

23. K. O. Dike, *Trade and Politics* . . ., p. 66.

24. "Kiya" refers to Kien and not to Ockiya. Bishop Crowther records that in 1857 the kings of Nembe were: "Kien of one division of the town and Arisima of the other."

25. The "two kings" in this case are likely to have been Ockiya (died Dec. 13, 1879) of Ogbolomabiri, and Ebifa of Bassambiri.

26. De Cardi in Kingsley, *West African Studies*, says that for the purposes of comey assessments, two tons of palm kernel were equivalent to one ton of palm oil.

27. Sir John Kirk, *Report on the Disturbance at Brass*, p. 9.

28. T. O. Elias, *Nigerian Land Law and Custom* (London, 1951), p. 64. The case was Chief Young Dede *vs* African Association Ltd.

29. The following were named treaty towns: Abonnema, Bakana, Buguma, Bonny, Calabar, Nembe, Opobo, and Twon. Payment was to be made as follows:

Nembe Native Authority — 90 pounds for the benefit of the inhabitants of Nembe and Twon; Kalabari Native Authority — 420 pounds for Buguma, Abonnema, and Bakana; Bonny Native Authority — 450 pounds for Bonny; Opobo Town, Urban District Council — 500 pounds for Opobo; Calabar Urban District Council — 400 pounds for Duke Town, Henshaw Town, Archibong Town, and Cobham Town; Western Calabar Rural District Council — 140 pounds for Creek Town.

30. NA/E, Brassdist, File No. OW 398/29, vol. II, M.P. No. 122/1931/11/213 of July 30, 1935. From D. O. Degema to Resident, Owerri Province, with comments on the claims of Eremoni of Buoama.

31. Chief Willie Obasi was the author's maternal grandfather.

32. NA/E, Brassdist, File No. BR. 8/1917. Letter from the Commissioner, Warri Province, to the District Officer, Brass, dated August 17, 1915, says "Chief Cameroon's subsidy will be deleted from 1916 Estimates. He can draw the present amount up to December, 1915."

33. The material for 1889–91 was taken from a tabular statement signed by Mr. D. C. MacDonald, Vice Consul for Brass, and from a memorandum by W. Fosbery, dated March 8, 1911. On January 20, 1888, King Ebifa received a comey payment of £31. 10. 2d. From June 1889 to August 1891, he got a total of £34. 10. 6d. From August 1891 until his death in 1894, he was paid 30 pounds a year.

King Koko was paid 25 pounds arrears in August 1891, and a further £130. 15/– in September 1892. This sum was used to pay debts incurred by King Ockiya with the Rio Bento Kernel Company. After August 1891,

King Koko received a monthly payment of £2. 10/– or 30 pounds per annum.

34. A. F. F. P. Newns, "Memorandum on Brass Subsidies," paragraph 18.

35. In the Amain-Kien-Alagoa House, the subsidy passed from Chief Edmund Natebo to Joseph Alagoa to Edward Alagoa. In 1943, the government decided that the head of the Amain House and not of the new Alagoa House should receive payment.

The subsidy paid to Chief Felix Amabebe Smoke as head of Pegi House in 1896 passed, on his death, to David Kerema, head of Tamuno House, and has remained there.

A similar change occurred in the 1905 subsidy paid to Fatewari of Iboama House. It passed to James Spiff, head of the Ada Spiff House of Twon.

The subsidy received in 1905 by Kponi Igbeta as head of the Igbeta House was claimed by his son, Samuel Bonnie, in 1928. In 1940 Samuel Bonnie received government recognition for a new Bonnie House. The Igbeta House subsidy then became the property of the new House.

CHAPTER 6

1. Richard and John Lander, *Journal of an Expedition* . . ., II, 249.
2. M. Laird and R. A. K. Oldfield, *Narrative of an Expedition* . . ., p. 334.
3. A. Tepowa, "A Short History of Brass . . .," pp. 47–49. Tepowa puts Kulo's death at 1860 instead of 1832.
4. R. and J. Lander, *Journal of an Expedition* . . ., II, 221, 253.
5. Laird and Oldfield, *Narrative of an Expedition* . . ., p. 334.
6. P. A. Talbot, *The Peoples of Southern Nigeria*, I, 251–53. Talbot gives King Opubu-Fubara's reign in Bonny as 1792–1837.
7. R. and J. Lander, *Journal of an Expedition* . . ., I, 235.
8. Laird and Oldfield, *Narrative of an Expedition* . . ., p. 313.
9. Laird and Oldfield, p. 314.
10. R. and J. Lander, *Journal of an Expedition* . . ., II, 237.
11. William Allen and T. R. H. Thomson, *A Narrative of the Expedition to the River Niger in 1841* (London, 1848), I 171.
12. Allen and Thomson, *A Narrative of the Expedition* . . ., I, 171.
13. Laird and Oldfield, *Narrative of an Expedition* . . ., p. 97.
14. R. and J. Lander, *Journal of an Expedition* . . ., II, 238.
15. W. B. Baikie, *Narrative of an Exploring Voyage* . . ., pp. 317–18.
16. Tepowa, "A Short History of Brass . . .," p. 49.
17. R. and J. Lander, *Journal of an Expedition* . . .," II, 250–52.
18. Thomas Hutchinson, *Ten Years' Wanderings Among the Ethi-*

opians (London, 1861), pp. 46–47. It is unlikely that Kien himself needed to go, or that the men involved were natives of Arochuku.

19. This is Rev. D. O. Ockiya's version. Tepowa says the war was the result of King Kien sacrificing Kalabari men in religious rituals.

20. K. O. Dike, *Trade and Politics* . . ., p. 187.

21. Tepowa, "A Short History of Brass . . .," p 50.

22. NA/E, Brassdist 1/82, pp. G88–H88.

CHAPTER 7

1. John E. Flint, *Sir George Goldie and the Making of Nigeria*, pp. 187–215. This gives an account of the events leading to the attack on Akassa.

2. Foreign Office Publication, Conf. 5913 of March 1890.

3. J. E. Flint, *Sir George Goldie* . . ., pp. 188–96.

4. Enclosure in Despatch No. 9, letter from King Koko and chiefs of Brass to Sir Claude MacDonald, February 4, 1895.

5. Enclosure in Despatch of May 1, 1895, MacDonald to Kimberley, letter from King Koko and chiefs of Brass to Sir Claude Macdonald, March 26, 1895.

6. NA/I, CSO, 1/11/5, Niger Coast Protectorate Despatches to the Foreign Office, Despatch No. 9 of 1895.

7. NA/I, CSO 1/11/5, Enclosure in Despatch No. 9, Joseph Flint, agent general, to C. E. Harrison, acting vice-consul, January 28, 1895.

8. NA/I, CSO 1/11/5, Enclosure in Despatch No. 9, Flint to Harrison.

9. Sir John Kirk, *Report on the Disturbances at Brass*, p. 27.

10. Kirk, *Report on the Disturbances at Brass*, p. 27. The priests claimed that the "heavy mist" was an additional protection provided by Ogidiga.

11. Enclosure in Despatch No. 9, Report by acting vice-consul C. E. Harrison, February 5, 1895.

12. Rev. D. O. Ockiya, "History of Nembe."

13. NA/I, CSO 1/11/5, Despatch No. 9 of 1895, MacDonald to Foreign Office, p. 40.

14. Kirk, *Report on the Disturbances at Brass*, p. 26.

15. Enclosure in Despatch No. 9, Report by acting vice-consul.

16. Enclosure in Despatch No. 9, Report by Father Bubendorfer.

17. Chief Christopher Warri was Christian, but there is no evidence that all the other chiefs were practicing Christians. In any case, none of them gave adherence to the Christian faith as their reason for abstaining. They were, rather, humane people who were brave in war, but who recoiled from the cold-blooded killing of prisoners — even in ritual sacri-

fice. King Ikata acted the same way in the Bila War, long before the coming of Christian missions.

18. Enclosure in Despatch No. 9, Report by Father Bubendorfer.

19. Rev. D. O. Ockiya, "History of Nembe," chapter entitled "The Akassa Raid, January 29th 1895."

20. Despatch, MacDonald to Lord Kimberley, April 30, 1895.

21. Mr. Bedford of the Royal Niger Company stated at the Kirk Inquiry (p. 20 of the Report) that during a visit to Akassa before the raid, Chief Spiff had said, "he would go where-ever he wishes in the territories, and would take out no permit or license. This he did."

22. NA/I, Niger Coast Protectorate Despatches, Despatch No. 10, MacDonald to Foreign Office.

23. Despatch No. 10.

24. Despatch No. 1, MacDonald to Foreign Office, Feb. 28, 1895. All citations on the fighting at Nembe are from this despatch.

25. Rev. D. O. Ockiya, "History of Nembe." He was an eyewitness of the fighting off Sacrifice Island from Chief Daniel Opuene's war canoe.

26. MacDonald to Kimberley, Despatch of May 1, 1895.

27. MacDonald to Kimberley, May 1, 1895.

28. Despatch of May 1, 1895. The owners of the two houses blown up were "Chiefs Okiye and Opuene." The first name is not known in Twon. In any case they are not included among the names of prominent chiefs who took part in the war.

29. Kirk, *Report on the Disturbance at Brass*, p. 26.

30. Despatch No. 1, MacDonald to Foreign Office, Feb. 28, 1895.

31. MacDonald to Kimberley, May 1, 1895.

32. MacDonald to Kimberley, May 1, 1895.

33. J. E. Flint, *Sir George Goldie . . .*, p. 211. Dr. Flint used the confidential manuscript version of Kirk's report at the Public Records Office, London, which contains material not included in the published Command Paper No. 7977 used here.

34. Draft Despatch No. 18, Moore to Foreign Office, March 13, 1896. King Koko's motive may have had something of what Sir Ralph alleges. But he may have also been genuinely afraid of being treated as King Jaja of Opobo had been in 1887.

35. Draft Despatch No. 29, Moore to Foreign Office, April 9, 1896.

36. Foreign Office Despatch No. 179, Chamberlain to Moore, Sept. 13, 1899. The terms of the compensation were given in an enclosure as "A Treasury Minute of 30th June 1899." The right to half of mineral royalties in Northern Nigeria was given up by the United Africa Company, successor of the Royal Niger Company, in 1947.

CHAPTER 8

1. NA/E, Brassdist, File No. W.597/1920.
2. Sir John Kirk, *Report on the Disturbances at Brass*, p. 27.
3. NA/E, Brassdist, File No. BR.27/28, meeting of A.D.O. with chiefs of Ogbolomabiri, Sept. 28, 1933.
4. Rev. D. O. Ockiya, "History of Nembe."
5. Draft Despatch No. 9 of 1895, MacDonald to Foreign Office.
6. Kirk, *Report on the Disturbances at Brass*, Enclosure D, p. 11.
7. De Cardi in Mary Kingsley, *West African Studies*, p. 478. This was the same de Cardi who was a member of the court of equity, Brass River.

SELECTED BIBLIOGRAPHY

Allen, William, and T. R. H. Thomson. *A Narrative of the Expedition to the River Niger in 1841*, 2 vols. (London, 1848).

Baikie, Dr. William Balfour. *Narrative of an Exploring Voyage up the Rivers Kworra and Binue (commonly known as the Niger and Tsadda) in 1854* (London, 1856).

Barbot, John. *A Description of the Coasts of North and South Guinea* (Paris, 1732).

Bosman, William. "A New and Accurate Description of the Coast of Guinea, Letter XX of Sept. 1, 1702, from David Nyendacl," in John Pinkerton, *A General Collection of the Best and Most Interesting Voyages*, vol. 16 (London, 1814).

Burton, Sir Richard F. *Wanderings in West Africa from Liverpool to Fernando Po* (London, 1863).

Cardi, C. N. de. "A Short Description of the Natives of the Niger Coast Protectorate, with some Account of their Customs, Religion, Trade, etc.," Appendix I in Mary H. Kingsley, *West African Studies* (London, 1899).

Dike, K. Onwuka. *Trade and Politics in the Niger Delta, 1830–1885* (London, 1956).

Flint, J. E. *Sir George Goldie and the Making of Nigeria* (London, 1960).

Hastings, A. C. G. *Voyage of the Dayspring, being the journal of the late Sir John Hawley Glover, together with some account of the Expedition up the Niger River in 1857* (London, 1926).

Hutchinson, Thomas. *Ten Years' Wandering Among the Ethiopians* (London, 1861).

Kirk, Sir John. *Report on the Disturbances at Brass,* Africa No. 3 (1896) [C. 7977].

Laird, Macgregor, and R. A. K. Oldfield. *Narrative of an Expedition into the Interior of Africa, by the River Niger, in the steam vessels Quorra and Alburkah in 1832, 1833 and 1834* (London, 1837).

Lander, Richard and John. *Journal of an Expedition to Explore the Course and Termination of the Niger with a Narrative of a Voyage Down that River to Its Termination,* 2 vols. (London, 1834).

Leonard, Arthur Glyn. *The Lower Niger and Its Tribes* (London, 1906).

Ockiya, Rev. D. O. "History of Nembe," n. d., unpublished MS at National Archives, Enugu.

Talbot, Percy Amaury. *The Peoples of Southern Nigeria,* 4 vols. (London, 1926).

—— *Tribes of the Niger Delta* (London, 1930).

Tepowa, Adebiyi. "A Short History of Brass and Its People," *Journal of the African Society* (now *African Affairs*), 1907.

Ukelonu, O. *Report of the Commission of Inquiry into the Nembe Chieftancy Dispute,* Official Document No. 24 (Enugu, 1960).

Archival Sources

National Archives of Nigeria, Ibadan (NA/I).
    Consular Records of the Provincial Office Calabar:
        Court of Equity, Brass River
        Despatches of the Niger Coast Protectorate.
National Archives of Nigeria, Enugu (NA/E).
    Records of the District Office, Brass (Brassdist).
    Records of the District Office, Degema (Degdist).
Dickinson, E. N. An Intelligence Report on the Nembe Clan, 1932.
Intelligence Reports, Okrika, 1933, no author.
Newns, A. F. F. P., Intelligence Report on the Akassa Clan, 1935.

INDEX